Managing Anxiety With Mindfulness

FOR
DUMMIES®
A Wiley Brand

by Joelle Jane Marshall

FOR
DUMMIES®
A Wiley Brand

Managing Anxiety With Mindfulness For Dummies®

Published by: **John Wiley & Sons, Ltd.**, The Atrium, Southern Gate, Chichester, www.wiley.com

This edition first published 2015

© 2015 John Wiley & Sons, Ltd, Chichester, West Sussex.

Registered office

John Wiley & Sons Ltd, The Atrium, Southern Gate, Chichester, West Sussex, PO19 8SQ, United Kingdom

For details of our global editorial offices, for customer services and for information about how to apply for permission to reuse the copyright material in this book please see our website at www.wiley.com.

Wiley publishes in a variety of print and electronic formats and by print-on-demand. Some material included with standard print versions of this book may not be included in e-books or in print-on-demand. If this book refers to media such as a CD or DVD that is not included in the version you purchased, you may download this material at www.dummies.com. For more information about Wiley products, visit www.wiley.com.

Designations used by companies to distinguish their products are often claimed as trademarks. All brand names and product names used in this book are trade names, service marks, trademarks or registered trademarks of their respective owners. The publisher is not associated with any product or vendor mentioned in this book.

LIMIT OF LIABILITY/DISCLAIMER OF WARRANTY: WHILE THE PUBLISHER AND AUTHOR HAVE USED THEIR BEST EFFORTS IN PREPARING THIS BOOK, THEY MAKE NO REPRESENTATIONS OR WARRANTIES WITH THE RESPECT TO THE ACCURACY OR COMPLETENESS OF THE CONTENTS OF THIS BOOK AND SPECIFICALLY DISCLAIM ANY IMPLIED WARRANTIES OF MERCHANTABILITY OR FITNESS FOR A PARTICULAR PURPOSE. IT IS SOLD ON THE UNDERSTANDING THAT THE PUBLISHER IS NOT ENGAGED IN RENDERING PROFESSIONAL SERVICES AND NEITHER THE PUBLISHER NOR THE AUTHOR SHALL BE LIABLE FOR DAMAGES ARISING HEREFROM. IF PROFESSIONAL ADVICE OR OTHER EXPERT ASSISTANCE IS REQUIRED, THE SERVICES OF A COMPETENT PROFESSIONAL SHOULD BE SOUGHT.

For general information on our other products and services, please contact our Customer Care Department within the U.S. at 877-762-2974, outside the U.S. at (001) 317-572-3993, or fax 317-572-4002. For technical support, please visit www.wiley.com/techsupport.

A catalogue record for this book is available from the British Library.

ISBN 978-1-118-97252-6 (paperback); ISBN 978-1-118-97261-8 (ebk);
ISBN 978-1-118-97257-1 (ebk)

Printed in Great Britain by TJ International, Padstow, Cornwall

10 9 8 7 6 5 4 3 2 1

Contents at a Glance

Table of Contents

Introduction

● ●

*W*elcome to *Managing Anxiety With Mindfulness For Dummies.* Mindfulness has ancient roots in Buddhism and other religions but is now rapidly gaining recognition as a secular practice that can help manage and reduce chronic pain, depression and anxiety. It also has many other benefits such as greater joy in the present moment, better sleep quality and less stress.

Everyone experiences some difficulties over the course of their life, including anxiety. This is a natural and normal part of the human experience. Mindfulness offers a way of managing anxiety in an accepting and balanced way, so that when anxiety does arise, you will be able to realise it and manage it and watch it evaporate in its own time, without judging or forcing it to move away.

Mindfulness also helps you when your life is going well. You live more in the present moment, are more focused and less stressed, are kinder to yourself and those around you, more willing to forgive yourself when you make mistakes, have a greater connection to the world around you and are more grateful.

I've written this book to make managing your anxiety with mindfulness achievable in your life. There are explanations for what anxiety is and why we experience it and meditations that you can practice in your daily life. Some are short exercises and some are longer, so even with a busy life, they are easy to slot into a daily routine.

About This Book

In this book is some theory about anxiety and why we suffer from it, how mindfulness works to help manage it and a range of different exercises with explanations of how to do them. Mindfulness works best when it is practised by engaging in the meditations and exercises, so this book is great for not only understanding your own anxiety but also how to begin to implement mindfulness in your own life.

This book can be used as a guide for mindfulness exercises to help manage your anxiety. The informal mindfulness exercises mentioned in the book cover a wide range of common activities and can be done several times a day, while the more formal mindfulness meditations can be completed once or twice a day to get the maximum effects of mindfulness.

Anxiety is the main focus of this book as it looks at the main ways in which you can use mindfulness to overcome anxiety. However, the mindfulness exercises and tips are also useful if you are suffering from depression, stress or physical health conditions. Mindfulness is also great for improving creativity, allowing yourself to live more fully in the present moment and improving focus and concentration. It has benefits for everyone, not just those who are trying to manage conditions such as anxiety, stress or depression.

Foolish Assumptions

If you have picked up this book, I am assuming that you have heard about mindfulness and how it can help anxiety and want to know more. I am assuming that you want to learn a little bit about how the mindfulness exercises can help you. Lastly, I'm assuming that you want to begin to try mindfulness for yourself, formally, informally or both, which is where this book can help you.

You may have anxiety and are looking for a solution, you may be a therapist who is looking to understand more about mindfulness and use it to help your clients or you may be a concerned friend, relative or partner of someone who struggles with anxiety and would like to learn more about mindfulness in order to try and help. Whatever the situation, I hope this book will prove to be a helpful guide.

Icons Used in This Book

I use icons throughout this book to bring different types of information to your attention and to clearly guide you through the book.

This icon is used to remind you to keep certain things in mind as you go through the book.

The Tip icon can offer little additions to help you enhance a particular exercise or meditation.

This icon is used to help you to engage with mindfulness exercises.

This icon is an alarm that alerts you to common errors and possible dangers, and warns you to take care.

This little owl is an icon for stories and little pearls of wisdom.

Beyond the Book

Find out more about Managing Anxiety With Mindfulness by checking out the bonus content available to you at www.dummies.com.

You can locate the book's e-cheat sheet at www.dummies.com/cheatsheet/managinganxiety, where you'll find handy hints and tips.

Be sure to visit the book's extras page at www.dummies.com/extras/managinganxiety for further Managing Anxiety With Mindfulness-related information and articles.

Where to Go from Here

This book offers theory and some exercises to manage anxiety with mindfulness. Being a more of a theory book, I give more space to understanding anxiety and mindfulness and less to practising mindfulness. If you'd like a more practical approach to developing the mindfulness exercises and to experience some guided audio meditations, you may also like *Mindfulness Workbook For Dummies* by myself and Shamash Alidina (Wiley).

Part I

Getting Started with Managing Anxiety

In this part . . .

✔ Find out more about the common causes of anxiety.

✔ Discover just how anxiety affects your mind and your body.

Chapter 1

Peering into the World of Anxiety

*A*nxiety is very common. Everyone experiences some form of anxiety on a day-to-day basis. It can be a helpful emotion, making you focused, alert and productive, but it can also be incredibly upsetting, uncomfortable and hard to live with.

In this chapter, I describe the nature, experience and symptoms of anxiety, show how it can affect your body and mind and help you discern whether your levels of anxiety are severe or normal. I also introduce you to mindfulness – what it involves and how it can help when battling anxiety – including a short mindfulness exercise for you to try.

Comparing Fear, Excitement and Anxiety

Fear, excitement and anxiety are all common emotions. All three can conjure the same feelings, but crucial differences exist between them. Fear and excitement can be helpful emotions, whereas anxiety can sometimes result in a lot of discomfort. In this section, I explain the differences between these three feelings.

Investigating fear

Fear is a natural emotion, as is anxiety. In fact, fear raises the same feelings that anxiety can, such as alarm or apprehension. The difference is that with fear, these feelings have a reason behind them.

Fear is a feeling of terror, distress or alarm caused by a danger or a threat. For example, you may feel fear when you see a car racing toward you at great speed, when you're in a situation where you may slip and fall or when you see a snake.

Clarifying the difference between anxiety and excitement

Feeling emotions such as agitation and distress without a just reason is one of the main factors of anxiety.

Anxiety is similar to fear, but without any obvious danger. It's a thought focused on something going wrong in the future and is often a notion that things are worse than they really are. Sometimes a traumatic event or lots of stress-causing factors trigger anxiety, but other times it doesn't have an identifiable reason. For more on the causes of anxiety, check out Chapter 2.

Anxiety is in the present moment, but the reason for it isn't always clear – unlike with fear.

Everyone on the planet experiences some level of anxiety at some point – it's a natural part of the human experience! But if you're finding your anxiety difficult to deal with, don't worry: Anxiety can be a very treatable condition.

In the physical sense, excitement is very similar to anxiety. If you're excited about something, you may recognise the same physical sensations, such as a fast heartbeat and sweating.

Although excitement can arouse the same physical reactions as anxiety, the difference is internal. Feeling excited creates positive thoughts of future or past experiences, conjuring up positive outcomes, such as feelings of happiness connected to your social life.

If you're anxious, however, you may be waking up every day with the same sense of dread but no real reason for it. Perhaps you're avoiding certain social situations or activities, even though you know that doing so is silly. Check out Table 1-1 for a comparison of fear, anxiety and excitement.

Table 1-1	Differences between Fear, Excitement and Anxiety	
Emotional State	*Physical Sensations*	*Reasons*
Fear	Fast heartbeat, sweating, high energy	An immediate threat of danger
Excitement	Fast heartbeat, sweating, high energy	Can originate from or lead to positive memories
Anxiety	Fast heartbeat, sweating, high energy	Something that may happen in the future, which is causing worry and stress; or for no clear reason at all

Discovering the Effect of Anxiety on the Mind

The mind expresses anxiety through worry, which often conjures up a collection of images, thoughts and feelings. One of the main anxiety problems that people experience is uncontrollable, excessive worries about anything, from minor to major things, despite no real threat of danger.

Your worries can take the form of several types of disturbing thoughts and feelings, such as the following:

✔ Thinking that you may lose control (go mad)

✔ Feeling detached from the world around you

✔ Thinking that everyone is everyone is watching you and knows that you're anxious

✔ Wanting to run away to avoid the situation

✔ Visiting the doctor often with irrational worries about your health (for example, thinking that you have cancer or a brain tumour)

✔ Feeling hypersensitive and hyper alert to everything around you

As well as the worrying, anxiety can also affect your mind in other ways:

✔ Feeling irritable

✔ Feeling fearful

✔ Lacking the ability to concentrate

✔ Needing reassurance desperately

✔ Feeling dependent

✔ Feeling depressed

✔ Losing confidence

Anxiety is provoked by thoughts about fear rather than an immediate danger, and so the meaning that the brain gives the thought is all about perception. For example, you may have stumbled in a job interview just once, but the brain remembers this event as an unpleasant experience, which then creates anxiety. Other people may have also stumbled at previous job interviews but did well at the next ones; their brains didn't let the unpleasant experience take over.

Read Chapter 4 for more on how thoughts affect your mind and body.

Finding out the Physical Effects of Anxiety on Bodily Functions

As I describe in the earlier section 'Clarifying the Difference between anxiety' and excitement, the physical effects on the body from anxiety are similar to the effects evoked from fear or excitement:

✔ Heart pounding

✔ Rapid breathing

- ✔ Urgency to use the toilet more often
- ✔ Pins and needles
- ✔ Dizziness
- ✔ Sweating
- ✔ Feeling sick
- ✔ Tense muscles (especially in the chest area)
- ✔ Dry mouth
- ✔ Headaches

Chapters 3 and 5 describe how mindfulness meditations can ease your physical health.

Understanding the Fight-or-Flight Response

The fight-or-flight response goes back to the days of cave dwellers and is the body's natural reaction to danger. A researcher called Walter B Cannon discovered in 1915 that animals experience physical changes when confronted with danger. He found that the increases in blood pressure, secretion of powerful hormones and other physical and psychological changes prepare the animal to *fight or flight*.

Humans experience this same response to danger. Fight-or-flight is useful when people need to defend their families against wild animals, save them from burning buildings or run from a danger they can't fight off, such as a natural disaster. But when you're just doing day-to-day things, such as going to the shops, commuting to work or looking after children, this sudden release of hormones and physical changes can be difficult to deal with.

The excess chemicals that your body releases aren't needed. As a result, the decreased carbon dioxide level in your lungs and blood can make you feel dizzy or faint, causing you to hyperventilate, which is when a panic attack can occur.

Exploring Why Thinking Negatively Is a Natural Human Trait

Your brain is more likely to think negatively rather than positively for one simple reason: survival.

If people thought positively all the time, they wouldn't have a natural awareness to danger, and the human race wouldn't have survived! If cave dwellers had just chilled out all the time, enjoying their cave paintings without a care in the world, the chances are that they'd have been killed and eaten by wild animals pretty quickly.

As a result, the brain is naturally wired to think more negatively than positively, and people are more likely to remember negative events than positive ones. The brain is also very quick at trying to create patterns, even if it has little evidence. It's your brain's way of protecting you from danger. The human nervous system is nervous.

Imagine that you stumbled during a work presentation a couple of times in the past – mixing up your notes, spilling your coffee and generally coming across like Mr Bean. The brain remembers these embarrassing events and creates a pattern for you, telling you that every time you have a work presentation, you'll mess up again. Or say that you've had two bad relationship experiences: Your brain can now tell you that all members of the opposite sex are useless.

But you're no longer a cave dweller. You don't need this pattern of negative thinking because danger is no longer as imminent as it was thousands of years ago. With no real threat of present danger, these patterns can result in anxiety.

What used to be a saber tooth tiger is now more likely to be a paper-tiger.

It's noteworthy to learn that humans can turn on the stress response by their thoughts alone, which can have the same measurable effects as any threatening stressor in the environment.

Recognising Whether Your Anxiety Is Normal or Severe

Anxiety of some degree affects everyone at some point. In general, anxiety comes in two levels:

- ✔ **Mild or everyday:** For example, being worried about an upcoming exam, work presentation or a medical test.

- ✔ **Severe or excessive:** For example, chronic worrying with no real reason that severely affects your life and having difficulty remembering the last time you felt relaxed.

I help you discover your personal anxiety levels in Chapter 10.

Suffering from excessive anxiety

High anxiety levels can be very unhelpful, interfering with your daily life and function. Here are some attributes of high or excessive anxiety:

- ✔ Doesn't have a known reason or only a very vague one

- ✔ Very intense, well beyond everyday anxiety

- ✔ Lasts much longer than everyday anxiety, perhaps weeks or months

- ✔ Has an unfavourable impact on living, perhaps leading to unhelpful and addictive behaviours, such as consuming drugs or alcohol, avoidance or withdrawal as ways of coping.

Sometimes you can have very high levels of anxiety without having an anxiety disorder that can be long term, such as Generalised Anxiety Disorder (GAD). This is normal and can be caused by stressful and traumatic life events, such as a divorce, moving house, the loss of a loved one and other big life changes, which can create anxiety feelings. Mindfulness can help with this because it teaches you to be an observer of your experience rather than feel attached to it. So when life gets a little difficult, you can better manage any anxious feelings that may arise.

Accepting that mild anxiety can be helpful

Mild anxiety that you don't find debilitating can be useful. Everyone worries, and as long as it isn't excessive, it can be a good thing. Anxiety increases your attention and so can enhance productivity and performance. If I didn't have any anxiety whatsoever, I'd never get this chapter written! But I know that I have a deadline looming, and so my brain is kicking me into action to get writing and working. Otherwise, I'd still be at home lounging about!

Here are some other examples of mild anxiety being helpful: just before you go to speak in public; before you participate in any competitive sport; before you take an exam; and before you hand in an important piece of work for a qualification or a work presentation.

Your anxiety keeps you focused by increasing your attention, allowing you to stay productive and get the job done.

Examining two common experiences of anxiety

Here's an example of how one event can spiral anxiety out of control.

Janet was feeling unwell one day and got on a train at a busy time when everyone was leaving work. On this train, she started feeling really sick and then fainted suddenly. Other people on the train looked after her and a friend met her to take her home, but she kept remembering the unpleasant event on that train home from her work. She started to take a different route to work and leave later so that the train wouldn't be as busy. She then started cutting down her hours at work, leaving the house when it was less busy on her route to work. Eventually, she started to work from home, fearful of other commuters and public transport and refusing to leave the house.

No evidence supported the idea that Janet was going to get sick and faint on a train again, but her anxiety took over and stopped her from doing her daily commute that she was so used to.

In this next common experience of anxiety, a stressful event arises, and the brain goes into overdrive.

Adam was a bright and intelligent student. He enjoyed learning and getting involved in projects. He was creative and contributed a lot to whatever group he worked with. However, when exam time arrived, he suffered terrible anxiety. It took over his brain, and he found himself stressed, under pressure and unable to concentrate on studying. He started to panic about the lack of study that his anxiety was stopping him from doing, thus making the anxiety worse.

The more Adam started to worry about his anxiety causing these issues, the worse it got.

Applying Mindfulness to Your Anxiety

It is common sense to take a method and try it. If it fails, admit it frankly and try another. But above all, try something.

—Franklin D Roosevelt

Scientific studies show that the development of a regular mindfulness practice can improve the way you experience life. With regular practice, you may feel less stressed, better equipped to deal with difficult situations, feelings or emotions, including your anxiety, and more focused and healthier as a result.

Chapter 7 goes into much more detail about your journey away from anxiety with mindfulness.

Defining mindfulness

In its simplest form, *mindfulness* means paying attention to whatever's happening now in a nonjudgemental way. It involves being aware of your present-moment experience without judgement while using compassion (see Chapter 6), curiosity (Chapter 4), acceptance and openness for yourself, other people and the world around you. You practise mindfulness with daily meditations and by living mindfully day-to-day (as I discuss in Chapter 8). I also describe ten productive mindful attitudes to remember in Chapter 12.

Set aside a couple of minutes for this exercise, which shows how it is possible to be mindful anywhere and at any time just using your awareness to be in the present moment:

1. **Take three deep breaths, holding each one for around 5 to 10 seconds.**

2. **Feel the weight of your body on the seat (if you're sitting) or your feet on the floor (if you're standing).**

3. **See whether you can feel any sensations with the part of the body that has contact with the floor or the seat.**

   If you can't feel anything, that's okay and perfectly normal. Just be aware of the lack of sensation if you can.

4. **After a few moments, gently open your eyes.**

If your mind wanders off to other things during the meditation, don't worry; this is perfectly normal and is the nature of the mind. Just gently bring your attention back to the sensation of your body on the floor or chair.

When you're focusing on the sensation of your body sitting or standing, you're bringing yourself into the present moment. This experience is what's happening right now, such as when you're standing or sitting to read this book. I provide a specific sitting meditation in Chapter 5.

Mindfulness sounds simple in theory, but the tricky bit in practice is trying not to react automatically. You may be self-critical when you first start practising, but that's quite usual. For suggestions on staying motivated, flip to Chapter 9.

Mindfulness isn't a new concept, but it's rapidly gaining popularity in the Western world of psychology. Many people associate mindfulness with Buddhism, but it also has roots in Hinduism and other religions. You don't have to be religious to practise mindfulness. It's accessible to all – religious, agnostic or atheist.

Discovering how mindfulness can help your anxiety

Mindfulness can help reduce your anxiety in a number of ways:

- ✔ **Moving toward your feelings rather than avoiding them.** If you're suffering from anxiety, the likelihood is that you try to avoid your feelings. This response is normal because you're trying to protect yourself from unpleasant feelings. But doing it can further increase your anxiety because avoidance comes from a place of fear that also creates anxious feelings. Mindfulness shows you how to approach and accept your feelings bit by bit, thus creating a healthier relationship with your anxiety.

- ✔ **Refusing the notion that you're just your anxiety.** You may believe that your anxiety has control over and is a part of you. Mindfulness shows you how to observe thoughts, feelings and emotions without identifying with them. Therefore, it shows you that you aren't your anxiety. When you separate from the feelings, you can observe them arising and possibly disappearing, too.

- ✔ **Being aware of unhelpful automatic thoughts.** When you become mindful, you start to become aware of unhelpful thought patterns that do nothing to serve you in a positive way. When you notice these patterns, you can shift your attention to something else, such as focusing on your breathing, the sensations in your feet or the task in hand.

- ✔ **Withstanding difficult physical sensations or emotions.** When you practise mindfulness regularly, you become better at simply being with difficult experiences without reacting to them. When you become able to 'sit with' your anxiety in this way, you're less likely to make the feeling worse.

- ✔ **Giving you back a sense of control.** Mindfulness allows you a moment of choice about how you react to a feeling. As a result, you begin to feel in control, which can positively reduce your anxiety.

For ten quick meditations for anxiety, turn to Chapter 11.

Positive mindfulness research

Positive research shows that mindfulness is useful for tackling anxiety. Researchers held an eight-week mindfulness course for a small group of patients with Generalised Anxiety Disorder (GAD). This is a long-term condition that causes excessive anxiety across a wide number of situations and issues rather than being linked to a specific event. Researchers found significant reductions in anxiety and panic immediately after the course, after three months and even after three years. Many of the patients continued to practise mindfulness, finding it helpful.

Another interesting form of therapy that uses mindfulness is called ACT (Acceptance and Commitment Therapy). Developed in the 1980s, research seems to show that ACT is effective for a range of disorders including, but not limited to, social anxiety, depression, obsessive compulsive disorder (OCD), borderline personality disorder, workplace stress, chronic pain, weight control, diabetes management and stopping smoking. ACT helps you accept what's out of your personal control and commit to action that improves your life, as follows:

✓ Using mindfulness skills to deal with difficult thoughts and emotions

✓ Helping you determine your values (discovering what's truly important to you) and offering ways to help you move toward living by your values

Mindfulness within ACT comprises four principles:

✓ **Defusion:** Using techniques to let go of difficult thoughts, memories and beliefs. *Fusion* means to be stuck, so *defusion* is about becoming unstuck, seeing that thoughts are just images and sounds in the mind. Here's one of many ways to defuse: If you find yourself thinking, 'I'm rubbish at this', for example, you imagine that sentence in front of you with curiosity. Then you imagine Mickey Mouse repeatedly saying those words in a high-pitched voice. Finally, you imagine the character dancing around and saying, 'I'm rubbish at everything'.

✓ **Acceptance:** Allowing painful sensations, thoughts, feelings and emotions without struggling against them. It doesn't mean giving up or admitting defeat or thinking that the feeling will last forever (a common misconception about acceptance in mindfulness – see Chapter 3 for more on such errors). It just means letting go of the fight with your present-moment experience.

✓ **Present moment:** Being in contact with the here and now experience with curiosity and a sense of openness.

✔ **Observing yourself:** Stepping back and observing your experience without identifying with it. This approach means watching thoughts and emotions as they arise as an observer or witness instead of them being part of you. The ACT approach is different from the mindfulness approach mainly in that the focus is on action and less on longer mindfulness meditations. The idea is to use mindfulness skills as you move toward your goals, which are based on your values.

Trying out a mindful exercise

You can use this practical exercise, known by the acronym STOP (Bob Stahl Ph.D. and Elisha Goldstein, PhD, *A Mindfulness-Based Stress Reduction Workbook*), to manage your anxiety when it arises:

1. Stop

If you're in the middle of work or something else, take the time to stop. If you really don't think that you can stop, you really do need to stop!

If you're at work or in a social situation, excuse yourself to the bathroom or somewhere where you know you can get some peace for a few minutes. Stopping may not be easy, but it has a positive effect.

2. Take some mindful breaths

Take a few slow, deep mindful breaths. Feel the breath as it moves down into your tummy. Make sure that your tummy is expanding as you breathe in and contracting as you breathe out. If it helps, place your hands on your tummy and concentrate on the breath pushing your hands out and then in.

You're moving your attention away from thoughts, emotions and bodily sensations and onto your breathing. If you can't feel your breath in your tummy, just focus on wherever you can feel it.

3. Observe

When you're ready, notice your bodily sensations. See whether you can shift your attention toward any physical discomfort that you may have and allow these sensations to be just as they are. Try to feel them together with your breathing. Bring a sense of kindness as you do so, instead of judgement.

Remember that feeling anxiety is quite natural. Use your breathing as a sort of rooted tree to help support your attention on any bodily discomfort. You can even try gently smiling toward your feelings, even if you don't feel like smiling. Then, after observing your body for some time, you can move on to emotions and thoughts. Just watch them and see whether they fade away in their own time, if they want to.

4. **Proceed**

Gently bring your attention back to whatever it was you were doing before you started this exercise. As you move your attention back to the outer world, try to give full attention to your senses instead of getting lost in thought. Continue your work or daily activities with a sense of acceptance and acknowledgement of your feelings as they are, knowing that all feelings are temporary and pass away in time.

Chapter 2

Finding Out the Common Causes of Anxiety

In This Chapter

▶ Discovering what can cause anxiety

▶ Letting go of identifying with anxiety

▶ Keeping modern life from increasing your anxiety

*I*n this chapter, I explore some of the more common causes of anxiety. Although no particular formula yet explains how anxiety arises in some adults, genetics, stress, environment and upbringing all play a role.

Even everyday living can play a part in affecting your anxiety. Just by making small changes, you may be able to decrease your stress, making your life a little easier and your anxiety more manageable.

Exploring Common Causes of Anxiety

Many different factors can contribute to your anxiety. You may recognize some of them as connecting to your personal experiences, and you may not. Sometimes anxiety can appear with no known reason, and sometimes you can easily identify its origin. Whether your anxiety has a known cause or not, you can still apply mindfulness throughout this book in the same way.

As you read this chapter, bear in mind that identifying with any of the experiences I mention doesn't mean you're doomed (*doomed,* I say, *doomed!*) to a lifetime of anxiety holding you prisoner. Anxiety is one of the most common mental health conditions, and many people may have had some of the same experiences you've had or are having. The fact is that you can manage your anxiety.

Anxiety in itself is a natural human emotion that everyone experiences from time to time. When I refer to anxiety, I'm talking about ongoing feelings of anxiety that negatively impact your ability to function in your work or home life.

Discovering your biology and your anxiety

Some research suggests that anxiety may be genetic in origin. You may notice that others in your immediate family or family tree have anxiety. But you can also have anxiety when no one else in your family does so. Anxiety is difficult to research because it can also be caused by other external factors that you and your family may all experience, such as difficult family relationships, low income or trauma of any kind.

Studies do show, however, that if you develop anxiety before the age of 20, close relatives, such as a parent or sibling, are more likely to have anxiety as well. In the case of twins, if one has a panic disorder, the other is more likely to develop a similar problem, too.

Experts haven't yet identified a specific gene that can cause anxiety. Other people with similar genes to you may not have developed anxiety because external factors, such as their environment, may be different. Much more research needs to be done to prove the genetic link and apply it to common therapies for anxiety.

The good news is that your brain and mind are malleable and can be trained. By using the meditations in this book, you can change your relationship with anxiety.

Finding out the stress factor

Some stress is normal. Everyone needs a little bit of stress to keep motivated and plan for the future. But chronic stress eventually leads to anxiety.

Chronic stress is basically emotional pressure that you endure for a long period of time and over which you feel you have no control. External factors that can lead to chronic stress are

- Work-related pressures
- Relationship troubles
- Family related-pressures
- Financial difficulties
- Social expectations

Lots of different issues can cause chronic stress, and sometimes you may not have a clear cause for it.

Internal factors can also cause chronic stress, such as not getting enough sleep, not having a nutritious diet and using illegal drugs or excessive amounts of alcohol to mute your stress.

These behaviours simply stop you from having a good coping mechanism to manage stress. Coping skills are vitally important when handling stress, and the use of drugs and high alcohol levels suppress them so that they don't work.

You can manage stress by changing your habits and lifestyle and by using meditation. Small changes, such as diet, sleep and making time for yourself, can make a big difference. Be kind to yourself and remember that you deserve not to be under constant stress – just like everyone else! Don't be afraid to ask for help if you need it and try not to take on too much in your home and working life. See Chapter 9 for more on healthy habits for better well-being.

Thinking causes most anxiety

Most anxiety is generated internally by your thinking – which doesn't mean that it's your fault! The human brain works in such a way that falling into negative thinking patterns is easy; it's the brain's vivid imagination about possible negative scenarios running away with itself.

Negative or worrying thoughts can spiral into a consistent stream of unhelpful thoughts, triggered by just one event. This behaviour is called *rumination*. Being a little worried about, say, your finances, an upcoming exam or starting a new job is perfectly normal, but if it becomes more severe than that, worrying rumination can adversely affect your life. Mindfulness training can help with rumination because it trains you to stay in the here and now rather than obsessing about future events,

Taking more severe anxiety as an example, you can see how normal events and thoughts that accompany those events can spiral out of control and cause anxiety. Check out the exact same scenarios in Tables 2-1 and 2-2 and compare the thoughts of people who don't have an anxiety condition (Table 2-1) with those who do (Table 2-2).

Table 2-1 Responses of a Nonanxious Person

Scenario	Thoughts of a Nonanxious Person
Your partner gets back late after going shopping.	'Maybe they saw a friend on the way home and stopped for a drink or a cup of tea or got delayed in traffic. They'll be home soon enough.'
A work colleague makes an unhelpful comment about the state of the economy.	'The economy is bad, but it won't be like this forever. Some great businesses have started in a recession.'
You watch a news article about a bombing in a distant country.	'This is sad, but it's far from me, and there's little I can do. I won't worry about it, but I'll look into contributing to an aid appeal for the victims.'
A friend doesn't call you back.	'Oh well, they're busy.'

The scenarios or external events are exactly the same, but the thinking in Table 2-2 can cause anxiety because the unhelpful thoughts can spiral out of control.

Table 2-2	Responses of an Anxious Person
Scenario	*Thoughts of an Anxious Person*
Your partner is late back from getting the shopping.	'They're late. Oh no, they must've had a car accident!'
A work colleague makes an unhelpful comment about the state of the economy.	'I'm going to get fired! They can't afford to keep me on in this economy! I'm going to lose my job, my house. What am I going to do?!'
You watch a news article about a bombing in a distant country.	'Oh, no, it's going to be us next! I'm not going to sleep tonight for thinking about it.'
A friend doesn't call you back.	'I knew they didn't like me. Why would they bother with me. I feel rejected and all alone.'

The good news is that mindfulness can help you identify anxious thinking patterns and so stop your thoughts spiralling. It can also help you to lose any self-identification with your anxious thoughts and be able to manage them more effectively. Check out Chapter 4 for more on this topic.

Understanding the Influences Affecting Your Anxiety

Identifying any social and emotional influences that may be contributing to your anxiety gives you a starting point to apply your mindfulness practice.

Considering the effect of childhood experience

Some childhood experiences can contribute to anxiety conditions in adults. Although the specific causes of anxiety aren't known, a link does exist between what happens in childhood and developing anxiety as an adult. If you had a parent with anxiety, for example, you're more likely to experience anxiety yourself. But whether that's down to a genetic link, you copying the anxious behaviour of the adult as a child or a mixture of both is still unclear.

Other childhood experiences that can cause anxiety are alcoholism in the family, child abuse, an overly critical parent, an overly protective parent, suppression of a child's feelings and separation from a parent. The more of these experiences a child is exposed to, the greater the risk of that child developing an anxiety disorder as an adult.

No doubt you can see where the anxiety stems from in some of these experiences. For example, in the case of an overly protective parent, the child grows up learning to fear the world and not being able to handle adversity, which, of course, is a normal part of life. In the case of an overly critical parent, the child grows up fearing that he can do nothing right and therefore develops anxiety.

The good news is that the human brain isn't static and rigid; you can change and reprogramme it. You can unlearn any negative childhood conditioning with time, practice and patience.

Exploring self-perception's impact on anxiety

Your *self-perception* – that is, how you see yourself and what you think and feel about yourself – is vitally important. Most people are unaware of the stream of thoughts that go through their head every day and the kind of self-talk that they're inadvertently listening to.

For example, do you find yourself berating yourself for little things that go wrong in your life and blaming yourself for everything? In the case of social anxiety, you may automatically jump to conclusions about what other people think of you. When you're in a social situation, you assume that they're thinking the worst of you, judging your looks, clothing and behaviour as if something's wrong with you.

The thoughts that cause this kind of negative self-talk aren't factual, of course. When you become aware of your thinking patterns with mindfulness, you can make better decisions on how to behave, react and gain more confidence.

Most people are their own worst critics. You need to accept that just because you see yourself in a certain way that doesn't mean everybody else does, too. It's just your thoughts that make it seem so. (See the nearby sidebar 'It's a branch! No, it's a rope! Nonsense, it's a pipe!' for an illustration of this subjective experience.)

Refusing to identify yourself with anxiety

You may identify with your anxiety by saying things such as 'I am anxious' or 'I am an anxious person'. In fact, you may often identify emotions as part of you instead of part of your experience.

The truth is that you are not your anxiety; it's only part of your experience, just as reading this chapter in this book is part of your experience. The body is a vessel in which thoughts and emotions come and go. You may house them for a little while, but they don't belong to you.

Religions such as Buddhism call this tendency to identify with your thoughts *attachment*. They suggest that instead you phrase such feelings as 'I'm with anxiety' rather than 'I am anxious'. Try it!

It's a branch! No, it's a rope! Nonsense, it's a pipe!

You may have heard one of the various versions of an ancient story about three blind men and an elephant. The first man touches the elephant's trunk, the second its tail and the third its tusk. Each man has a different experience of what an elephant is like because he's touching a quite different part. Their different – subjective – experiences mean that they all have a different perception of the elephant.

Your own self-perception is similarly subjective and works in the same way.

The problem with seeing your anxiety as part of you and not just part of your experience is that you further intensify it. For example, if you're going to visit your doctor for a simple checkup but have convinced yourself that you may have a life-threatening condition even though no evidence supports this thought, you can experience as much anxiety as if you did have a life-threatening condition. Similarly, if you're sitting on a plane and you experience some turbulence and you think 'The plane is going to crash', you may experience the same anxious thoughts and feelings as if the plane was going to crash!

You can read more about seeing yourself as separate from your anxious thoughts and feelings in Chapter 1's discussion on Acceptance and Commitment Therapy (ACT) and cognitive defusion.

Enjoying the benefits of socialising

Human beings are social animals, and lots of studies show that becoming social can improve your well-being. In modern-day living, people have smaller social circles and are often surrounded by fewer siblings and cousins, for example, because generally people tend to have smaller families.

The erosion of community, the breakdown of the extended family and the busy lives of nuclear families have all contributed to this.

People with few friends and limited social contact, such as not having a friendship network, may struggle with mental health problems such as anxiety. They don't have anyone to provide emotional support after suffering a stressful event, such as a job loss or bereavement.

Certain studies show that women suffering from an anxiety disorder who had positive social interactions, better access to information, help and emotional support generally had better psychological well-being. Other studies also show that women with someone to talk to after experiencing a stressful event are far less likely to develop a mental health condition, such as depression.

Being more social (whether conversing with acquaintances or engaging in friendship groups) also increases your brain's ability to process thoughts. Such interaction requires more concentration from you, more listening, maintaining a good memory and knowing when to reply in conversations.

Social engagement outside the family circle tends to have additional benefits because when you experience stress at home, receiving external emotional support is more beneficial.

Realising How Modern-Day Living Can Affect Your Anxiety

Living today is often fast-paced and instant, with people being bombarded with information every day in the form of words and images. But if you stop to analyse all this information, you soon discover that some of it is unnecessary and serves no purpose for you.

The overuse of certain technology and constant information can cause anxiety. Living a modern lifestyle without using it is difficult, however. In this section, I suggest ways to limit your use for less anxiety and better well-being.

Stopping negative media from affecting your anxiety

You absorb a lot of information day-to-day without even realising whether it's negative or positive. Thousands of good deeds happen in the world every day and yet go widely unreported and unnoticed: huge events such as scientific breakthroughs and cures for diseases, plus loads of small instances, such as a community coming together to do something good.

In November 2013 in San Francisco, the whole city was changed into Gotham City so that an ill little boy could fulfil his wish to be Batman for the day!

This story was reported, but most good deeds aren't. If you watch the news morning and night and read newspapers, you can easily come to believe that the whole world is negative and a horrible place to live.

Absorbing negative media all the time can affect your anxiety because you may start to fear events on the TV happening to you and lay awake worrying about them.

 If you're very anxious, avoid the negative news until you feel a bit better. If you can't do that, try not to watch it first thing in the morning because that sets up your day and last thing at night because you need to relax your body into sleeping mode. Also, stop reading beauty magazines because the unrealistic airbrushed images in them are unhelpful to self-acceptance and self-compassion, which is what you need to develop as part of managing your anxiety.

Another option instead of the mainstream news is to go online to www.TED.com, a nonprofit organisation dedicated to only hosting inspirational talks by people who are positively contributing to the world.

Reducing the adverse impact of technology on your anxiety

You may love your smartphone and browsing the Internet for hours on Facebook and Twitter, but doing so can cause anxiety and exacerbate existing anxiety conditions. Some studies show that the use of social media can heighten anxiety for two main reasons:

- **Social media can make you feel inadequate.** Your Facebook friends may be posting about their lives, their new houses, husbands, wives, children, jobs and amazing holidays. This bombardment makes you consistently compare your life to others and feel inadequate and not 'interesting enough' if you don't match up, which can cause feelings of anxiety.

- **Social media can isolate you.** The more time you spend at home online on social media, the less time you spend going out and enjoying quality time with friends in person. These relationships are very important when you're suffering with anxiety because you need their support and social connection. Spending too much time on Facebook people and the like can exacerbate social anxiety and increase your tendency to avoid people.

Social media can be very helpful if you're suffering from an anxiety condition, of course, because of all the many great communities and resources you can access online. But if you're suffering from anxiety, it's best to cut your social media online time down to just 30 minutes a day.

Everyone puts out on social media the image that they want you to see, not all the bad stuff. Therefore, you can easily think that everyone else has a perfect life except you, which isn't true!

Your phone can also cause anxiety. Having it switched on all day, where anyone can access you at any time, can be stressful because (like the phone!) you don't get to switch off and are constantly available. When a work email comes through, you feel compelled to answer it at any time of the day and night. Anxiety is caused by the demands of technology on you, when in fact it should help alleviate your stress.

Try combating this problem by switching off your phone for a couple of hours every evening. In that time, you can read, play with your children or do some of the exercises and meditations in this book undisturbed!

Part II

Learning More about Mindfulness for Anxiety

Discover your starting attitude

- ✔ What do you hope to get from mindfulness practice?
- ✔ What experiences do you expect to have with mindfulness?
- ✔ How long are you willing to try it for?
- ✔ What are your current thoughts on meditation?
- ✔ How much dedication will you devote to mindfulness?

For some online extras about Managing Anxiety with Mindfulness, head online and visit www.dummies.com/extras/managinganxiety.

In this part . . .

- ✔ Examine how your attitude can help ease your anxiety.

- ✔ Learn how managing your thoughts can lead to calmness.

- ✔ Find out more about mindful mediations.

- ✔ Use compassion and kindness to help prevent feeling anxious.

- ✔ Move from feeling anxious to a state of wellbeing using mindfulness.

Chapter 3

Discovering Mindful Attitudes Toward Anxiety

• •

In This Chapter

▶ Starting out with the right attitude

▶ Uncovering how mindfulness can benefit you

▶ Unearthing misconceptions about mindfulness

• •

> *Attitude is a little thing that makes a big difference*
>
> —*Winston Churchill*

*W*hen starting anything new, having the right attitude toward it is important because attitudes themselves can be helpful or unhelpful. If you start a practice such as mindfulness with a negative attitude, you're more likely to give up quickly and lose out on something that may potentially help you manage your anxiety.

In this chapter, I explain the many benefits of mindfulness, discuss helpful attitudes when practising it and dispel some myths about mindfulness itself.

Discovering Your Starting Attitude

When you begin with a positive attitude toward mindfulness, you're more inclined to keep up with the practice and so find an invaluable way to manage your anxiety. Therefore, discovering your feelings before you begin the practice is useful.

Get a pen and paper and write down your answers to the following questions. No right or wrong answers apply – just try to be as honest as you can so that you can gauge your attitude:

- ✔ What do you hope to get from mindfulness practice?
- ✔ What experiences do you expect to have with mindfulness?
- ✔ How long are you willing to try it for?
- ✔ What are your current thoughts on meditation?
- ✔ How much dedication will you devote to mindfulness?

Look at your answers. Are they positive, negative or in between? If they're negative, don't worry; you can change your attitudes.

Understanding the Benefits of Mindfulness

Mindfulness has been around for thousands of years but has only just started to become popular in the West and the field of psychology. Mindfulness contains lots of benefits, and research is discovering more all the time.

Let's get physical: Benefitting your health

Mindfulness helps you to check in or connect with your body and your mind, which can have significant positive effects. It can also help reduce the suffering of chronic pain in a range of illnesses and boost your immune system, too.

Here are some conditions for which mindfulness is being investigated as a treatment for the symptoms and associated pain:

- ✔ Cancer
- ✔ Chronic pain
- ✔ Diabetes

✔ Fibromyalgia

✔ Heart disease

✔ Hepatitis/HIV

✔ Hypertension (high blood pressure)

✔ Irritable bowel syndrome

✔ Postsurgical recovery

✔ Psoriasis

✔ Tinnitus

Research with and use of mindfulness reveals good success rates for some of these conditions. Others are in the early stages of research.

Don't use mindfulness to replace the existing medical treatments for any of the preceding conditions. Contact a medical professional before using mindfulness to see whether the person recommends using it alongside other medical treatments.

Mindfulness helps you connect with your body and become more aware of what's going on in the present moment instead of living on autopilot 24/7. Therefore, mindfulness can have the following positive effects:

✔ **Your mind begins to calm.** Your body is always in the present moment, which gives you a foundation on which to rest your focus.

✔ **You can start to deal with emotions.** Many people try to suppress emotions, such as anger, sadness and anxiety. Instead of suppressing them, mindfulness helps you work through them.

✔ **You react less automatically and negatively.** Whereas perhaps you used to react to certain situations with automatic anger or hypersensitivity, now mindfulness helps you choose how you react. Say, for example, someone cuts you up when you're driving, and your usual reaction is to beep your horn and shout. Mindfulness shows you how to notice the feelings in your body and choose your words and actions carefully, which can avoid landing you in a negative or aggressive situation.

✔ **You start to feel more grounded in your body, centred and present.** You start to enjoy the joy of the present moment more and feel more stable in yourself, aware of any sensations that may arise in your body. Instead of living in your head with thoughts elsewhere, you now can be aware of your body in the present moment.

✔ **You improve your focus and concentration.** Mindfulness meditation helps train your mind when it wanders. It allows you to focus on one thing at a time, such as your breath (check out the later section 'Introducing the Mindful Breathing Exercise'), and so helps you identify when your mind wanders and to guide it gently back to the point of focus. You can transfer this skill to other things in life as well as meditation, such as studying, driving or having a conversation. Therefore, you boost your overall focus and concentration on any task you have to do.

✔ **You increase your ability to be in a state of flow.** Following on from improving your focus and concentration, mindfulness also leads you toward a state of *flow*. Flow means being fully engaged in the task at hand, whether that's a leisure activity or a work task. Research shows that people who're in a state of flow a lot of the time are at their happiest. It allows them to have greater creativity and success in their work and personal lives.

Take me as I am: Appreciating the power of acceptance

Acceptance can be a misunderstood attitude as regards mindfulness meditation. If you have anxious feelings, thoughts and bodily sensations, you're more likely to try to avoid them automatically rather than accept them.

But avoiding your thoughts and feelings is hard work and can lead to more anxiety. This attitude has negative connotations because people believe that if they accept something, they're giving up or losing hope. In fact, accepting your anxious feelings as they are right now doesn't mean that they'll exist forever. In fact, allowing and accepting anxious feelings as they arise for you gives them the best opportunity to dissipate.

Open up your eyes: Focusing on an open mind

> *Nobody can go back and start a new beginning, but anyone can start today and make a new ending.*
>
> —*Maria Robinson*

To have an open mind is to be receptive to new ideas and be willing to give them a try. Open-mindedness is an important attitude in mindfulness because it may be a totally new way of living, thinking and existing for you.

Having an open mind is different from optimism, which is a way of imagining that things will always turn out well or positively, and pessimism, which is an attitude that always expects the worst to happen. To illustrate the difference, people often use the metaphor of a glass of water: pessimists tend to view the glass as half empty, whereas optimists view it as half full.

Mindfulness itself doesn't mean pessimism or optimism, but awareness. As a result, you discover how to notice pessimistic and optimistic attitudes to whatever you're doing. Mindfulness goes beyond the realm of thinking negatively or positively and sees thoughts in a neutral way. Therefore, even finding yourself to be a natural cynic is still a healthy attitude. As long as you cultivate an open mind, you have a chance to experience mindfulness and see the benefits of the practice for yourself. A closed mind or excessive scepticism is unhelpful and doesn't reveal the true effects of mindfulness.

Mindfulness isn't a magic cure. Being over-optimistic and believing that everything will work out perfectly the first time results in disappointment and can be detrimental to your practice. Be open-minded but realistic so that you don't become discouraged when things fail to go as smoothly as you want.

I've got the power!: Discovering the strength of the present moment

When you suffer from anxiety, you tend to worry about the future or future events. But the only moment you have is this one, right now. You're reading this book now, and that's your present-moment experience. Mindfulness encourages you to live in the present moment and to have an awareness of what's going on for you in the present moment.

Therefore, you notice and discover more about yourself, are more curious to the world around you and ultimately create a better future for yourself.

When you're aware of thoughts, emotions, body sensations and your senses, you're in the present moment. When you're worrying about the future or thinking about the past, you're no longer living in the present moment.

Here's one of my favourite poems about learning to enjoy the present moment:

> *What is this life if, full of care,*
>
> *We have no time to stand and stare.*
>
> *No time to stand beneath the boughs*
>
> *And stare as long as sheep or cows.*
>
> *No time to see, when woods we pass,*
>
> *Where squirrels hide their nuts in grass.*
>
> *No time to see, in broad day light,*
>
> *Streams full of stars, like skies at night.*
>
> *A poor life this if, full of care,*
>
> *We have no time to stand and stare.*
>
> *Songs of Joy and Others, 1911—WH Davies*

Of course, living every single moment in the present moment is impossible; you'd get nothing done! A little bit of forward thinking is needed daily, otherwise jobs such as planning dinner for the evening would prove difficult. You need to strike a balance.

Focusing on the present moment can help you deal with a lot of stressful events or things that seem overwhelming to you.

I have a friend who wanted to start writing a screenplay. The idea of producing enough material for a two-hour film was scary to him and felt like a mammoth task. However, a screenplay is roughly a page per minute of screen time, and so if he did ten minutes a day and committed to it, he could aim to have five to ten minutes of the screenplay written each day or thereabouts. If he remained present when he was focusing on just those ten minutes a day, the film would be written before he knew it.

In much the same way, you can break down stressful events or scenarios into small segments.

If you have difficulty managing your time, try small chunks of being present as you go through your day. Take one step at a time. For example, you can do small exercises to keep you in the present moment, such as this one:

1. **Eat breakfast and savour the flavour, smells and textures of your food (flip hungrily to Chapter 5 for more on mindful eating).**

2. **Feel the weight and connection of your feet on the ground as you walk to work or wherever you need to go.**

3. **Notice the smells, sounds and textures that are at your desk or at home.**

4. **Engage deeply with what other people are saying to you.**

5. **Note any positive connections with other people – for example, when someone holds a door open for you.**

6. **Enjoy deeply the pleasant moments that occur during the day with friends or family, such as your child bringing home a picture painted at school.**

7. **When you find yourself having an unpleasant feeling when interacting with another person, you can first acknowledge what you are feeling and then pause in the present.**

    This can be empowering because it gives you the time to respond instead of react.

We're absolute beginners: Seeing the world with a beginner's mind

Seeing things afresh is called using the *beginner's mind:* an approach that can help you view events in a new way. It's about letting go of every perception, idea and concept that you already have and trying to see things anew.

Children approach everything they encounter for the first time with new eyes and fascination. Have you ever watched a baby or a toddler see a new object or experience something for the first time? If it's an object, she's likely to want to touch it, taste it and maybe play with it. She wants to explore every inch of this object with interest and total absorption. If it's an experience, she may point excitedly at it, such as watching a kite dip and soar in the sky.

As the child gets more familiar with the experience and grows up, the object or experience is no longer exciting. The sun is just the sun, a pet is just a pet, a thunderstorm is just a thunderstorm and a balloon is just a balloon.

Mindfulness can help you reinvigorate your young child's brain and enjoy the amazing miracle of being alive. By being mindful, you begin to live in an exciting way as if everything in life is astonishing and wondrous.

This attitude is important because you begin to access a different mode of mind. If you're overwhelmed with anxiety, you're probably anxious about anxiety itself. By gently bringing a little kindness, curiosity and wonder to your life – whether it's cooking, walking or observing your thoughts and emotions – you start to unlock your frantic state of mind. Just take it slowly, step by step.

Of course, you can't live every single moment in this way. But a mindful attitude can help you see your anxiety in a different light or the causes of your anxiety with fresh eyes.

Challenging Preconceived Ideas about Mindfulness and Meditation

When you hear the word *meditation,* what's your general reaction? What springs to mind? Is it Zen Buddhist monks in robes sitting cross-legged on top of a mountain? Maybe spiritual gurus or hippies in flowing trousers with daisy chains in their hair and wreaths of flowers round their neck? Do you visualise yoga or t'ai chi practitioners in white linen suits?

People have lots of misconceptions about meditation and mindfulness meditation. Here are just a few:

✔ **You have to be a Buddhist.** Mindfulness has roots in Buddhism and Hinduism and other major religions, but you don't have to follow any of those religions or even believe in any religion to practise mindfulness. Mindfulness is a secular practice.

✔ **You have to clear your mind.** Mindfulness shows you how to develop a present-moment awareness and doesn't involve stopping thoughts or emotions. It's about learning to become aware of what's happening for you so that you can make wiser decisions on how to manage your experiences

✔ **You have to sit still for hours on end.** Although some mindfulness meditations involve sitting in a cross-legged position, you can bring mindfulness into your daily activities and even just to your breath. Mindfulness can slot into your daily life with ease.

✔ **Mindfulness is positive thinking.** Mindfulness is an awareness of what's going on for you, not about forcing yourself to feel or think a certain way.

✔ **Mindfulness is relaxation.** The ultimate aim of mindfulness isn't relaxation, although that may happen. Mindfulness meditation aims to increase your awareness, help you pay attention to the present moment and discover greater well-being.

Common Misconceptions

Mindfulness is rapidly gaining popularity in the West, and along with that comes a lot of hearsay about mindfulness and mindfulness meditation. Mindfulness can sometimes challenge any preconceived ideas about meditation and what you may be used to imagining when it comes to meditation practices.

In the following sections, I dispel some common misconceptions about certain aspects of mindfulness and mindfulness meditation.

Letting go of control doesn't mean giving up

> *Don't worry about the future; or worry, but know that worrying is as effective as trying to solve an algebra equation by chewing bubblegum.*
>
> —Baz Luhrmann

A lot of anxiety sufferers believe that they need their anxious and worrying thoughts because they help them feel like they're holding onto some kind of control. They may think that if they don't worry about certain situations or events, they lose power over trying to control the situation.

But you can't turn all worries or situations into problems that you can solve or control. For example, you may worry that you haven't found the person you want to spend the rest of your life with, or you don't know what you want to do with your life as regards a career. Although you can take steps to help with these things, you can't ultimately control them.

In such cases, anxiety is unhelpful, and you need to try to let it go. Doing so is scary, however, because you may equate letting go with giving up.

But in a mindfulness context, *letting go* (or *nonattachment*) is nothing to do with giving up. It's about letting go of the stress that doesn't serve you in any way, allowing you to have freedom from the constraints of controlling habits and thoughts.

For example, if you're having anxiety over an upcoming exam, letting go doesn't mean that you stop studying, give up and expect to fail. It means doing what you can, taking the steps you need to in order to prepare, but not attaching yourself to any anxiety you're suffering.

Anxiety is the illusion of control and doesn't help you pass your exam. Only the steps that you take can do that – in other words, lots of studying.

Practising meditation is for everyone

Mindfulness really is for everyone and anyone: young and old, male and female, working and not working, religious and nonreligious. For the basics of mindfulness, you just need yourself and your body and mind and a little time every day to practise. Even if you can't do the longer mindfulness meditations, you can still engage in plenty of short exercises and daily mindful tasks.

You don't have to have an interest in spiritual practices or psychology, and you can be from any walk of life. Although mindfulness started as an Eastern practice, experts brought it to the West, and now thousands of resources are available to you at the click of a button (see Chapter 10 for more information).

Here are some common reasons why people think that they can't take on mindfulness practice – and why they aren't true:

> ✔ **I don't have the time.** Actually, mindfulness can give you more time (say what!). It's true. Mindfulness helps improve your focus and concentration, and so you get more done because you concentrate better on the task in hand. Also, research shows that multitasking is bad for you and can reduce your productivity; the brain has only a limited capacity to focus on many things simultaneously.

✔ **I have a family to look after.** Mindfulness can incorporate and benefit the whole family, including children, and also help with parenting. Check out *Mindfulness Workbook For Dummies* (Wiley) by myself and Shamash Alidina for more details.

✔ **It's selfish.** When you get into a practice of mindfulness, you can reap its benefits, such as more enjoyment of life, more time in the present moment, increased focus and concentration and a better sense of well-being. The people around you surely benefit from that. Your family enjoys more time with you, your work colleagues benefit from your increased focus and concentration and you can help others more effectively. So, really, mindfulness is the opposite of selfish.

 Mindfulness is offered in a variety of workplaces, including large organisations such as Google. Check out your workplace and see whether it offers a mindfulness programme.

Viewing Mindfulness as a Way of Living

You can see mindfulness practice as coming in two forms, both of which fit into your everyday life:

✔ **Formal mindfulness:** Practising mindfulness meditations

✔ **Informal mindfulness:** Engaging in daily mindful activities

Do you brush your teeth every day and shower? I hope so! Then you can get into a habit of mindfulness in just the same way.

Mindfulness practice works best when you see it as a way of living and not as a temporary fix. The best results come when you take the time to meditate every day (even if you begin with just ten minutes) and perform daily mindful activities every day. Over time, you'll find that you get into a habit of practising and want to continue that habit because you recognise the benefits that mindfulness is bringing you. You may even use it in the most obscure of circumstances and find that it helps.

I once visited a restaurant in London that was pitch-black. I thought it would be a great new way of experiencing food with heightened senses: smells, taste and so on. When I got inside, however, I started to feel claustrophobic. I couldn't see my hand in front of my face, I had no idea how to get out if a fire started and I felt the stress response build in my body: faster heart rate, feeling slightly nauseous and so on.

The first thing I did was put my hands on the table and felt the texture of the table. I then listened to the surrounding sounds and engaged in conversation with a man next to me. My food came, and I focused on tasting it, trying to work out what each thing I put in my mouth was. I focused on my senses and slowly forgot about the claustrophobic feelings and enjoyed myself and my food. If I hadn't kept up with a long practice of mindfulness over time and found myself habitually using it to help me in a stressful situation, I may have left the restaurant and not enjoyed myself at all.

Introducing the Mindful Breathing Exercise

Mindful breathing is a basic but useful and effective mindfulness meditation. All you need is a quiet place to practise where you won't be disturbed for about 10 minutes. You can practise for a longer or shorter period of time if you want, but try ten minutes initially and then build on that time if you can.

Practising the mindful breathing exercise

This exercise is one of the most basic of mindful exercises but is still enormously valuable in your meditation practice. Try to bring an attitude of acceptance to whatever may happen in the practice,- as much as you can.

1. **Find a comfortable position.**

   Sit on the floor or a chair with your back straight and away from the wall or back of the chair. If you want to, close your eyes gently.

2. **Say to yourself that you're going to focus on your breathing.**

   Make a commitment to yourself that you'll try to focus on your breathing as best you can. I don't mean being harsh, critical or unkind to yourself if your mind wanders off to other thoughts (because it almost certainly will at first). Try to let go of the idea of doing this practice perfectly or achieving a certain goal. As best you can, simply aim to accept whatever outcome arises.

3. **Focus on your breathing.**

   Feel the breath wherever it feels easiest for you: back of the throat, the tummy, the chest or the nostrils. Focus on the breathing without forcing it to be a certain way. It may change, it may not: just focus on it as it is in the moment.

4. **Bring your mind back when it wanders off.**

   Your mind will wander off, which is perfectly natural. You may be thinking of to-do lists, dreams, hopes and worries. When you notice your mind has wandered off, gently bring it back to focusing on the breath. Try to do so without judging yourself. If you feel like you're getting annoyed at yourself, try a gentle smile and go back to the breath.

5. **Open your eyes after you finish practising.**

   Become aware of how you're feeling without judgement. Stretch out if you need to and continue with your day.

If focusing on your breath is too difficult and frustrating, try counting your breaths. Say 'one' on the in-breath and 'two' on the out-breath. Go up to ten and then start again at one. Whenever you lose focus, start again at one. Take your time and remember to feel your breath as you say the number in your mind – and be patient with yourself!

Enjoying the benefits of mindful breathing

Mindful breathing is simple but has great benefits. If you engage in mindful breathing over a long period of time, you're able to focus better in the present moment and therefore have less worry. (Anxiety can include worries about the future, and so present-moment awareness can redirect your focus.) Long-term practice of mindful breathing can also make you calmer, allow wider perspectives and raise your well-being levels.

Here are some other benefits of mindful breathing:

- ✔ It's easy because your breath is always available and accessible to you.

- ✔ It can help you notice when you're anxious, so you can catch your anxiety earlier and gently focus on your breath.

- ✔ Breath connects the mind to the body, and focusing on that connection can help to soothe your anxiety.

If you don't manage to practise any other meditation in this entire book but this one, you can still gain significant benefits. Keep a record of your practice and see how you feel after two months or so.

Chapter 4

Managing Your Thoughts Mindfully

In This Chapter

▶ Discovering the effects of anxious thoughts

▶ Attending mindfully to your thoughts

▶ Finding out that you don't have to believe your thoughts

*T*his chapter describes how to manage your thoughts mindfully. Mindfulness isn't about trying to stop unhelpful thoughts or suppress them so that you have a clear mind (to discover more misunderstandings about mindfulness, saunter to Chapter 3). Having a clear mind is impossible and because the mind is always active, trying to empty it can be highly frustrating. In contrast, mindfulness and mindfulness meditation show you how to accept any thoughts that arise and how to let go of identifying with them.

In this chapter, I describe how to manage your thoughts in different ways. You find out how to stop self-identifying with them and how to step back from them. You discover that different attitudes toward your thoughts can take away their control. I also introduce some mindful metaphors to help you detach yourself from your thoughts (which, remember, aren't necessarily facts) and instead simply notice them pass by.

Accepting That Thoughts Impact Your Mind and Body

Thoughts can have an impact on your mind and body, particularly if a pattern of anxious thoughts keeps ruminating around in your head. The human brain naturally leans toward the negative (as I describe in Chapter 1), and so thoughts can then repeat themselves continuously.

Imagine a record player with a stuck record. Thoughts can repeat in much the same way (imagine *The Birdie Song* (the *Chicken Dance*) going round and round forever – torture!).

Letting up on your mind

Anxious thoughts narrow your focus. Instead of having a wider perspective on things, you start to see things as more threatening than they are, even if they aren't threatening you at all.

For example, imagine someone coming up to you and asking how you are and you respond with 'What's your problem? Why do you keep asking me that?' The person may have had the best intentions, but you saw the words as a threat and so acted defensively.

Anxiety is a result of fearing fear itself, meaning you are nervous about what may befall you, even if there is no reason or direct threat toward you, so you start to see the fear itself as a threat and put avoidance tactics in place. But this response gives the anxiety more negative attention, and the fear levels increase.

In mindfulness, you start to learn to be more gentle and kind with yourself and understand that these anxious feelings will pass. Even the knowledge that you won't come to harm helps, such as when you fear that you're having a heart attack when you merely have a rapid heart rate or a panic attack.

Giving your body a break

In essence, the anxious thoughts that affect the body involve your stress response. These effects can manifest themselves in different ways. (Chapter 1 contains a full list.)

When you inadvertently activate the stress response, your immune system is boosted but then goes down. The reproductive system closes down, and digestion partially shuts down. Your body goes into a sort of emergency mode and uses only what it needs at that time so that no extra energy for anything else is expended.

Even though these anxious thoughts have an impact on your body and can be uncomfortable, they don't kill or harm you. Thoughts only ever have the power you give them.

Bringing Mindful Attention and Curiosity to Your Thoughts

Anxious thoughts can be unpleasant, and so unsurprisingly your initial reaction is to try to suppress or fight them. But bringing mindful attention to your thoughts allows you to better manage your stress response (see the preceding section), which helps thoughts lose their power and their ability to affect you.

You can use this exercise straightaway to relieve mild stress and anxiety. When you feel like you understand it fully, you can use it for more severe stress and anxiety. The easy way to remember this exercise is with the acronym RAIN:

   ✔ **Recognise:** Become aware of your current state of mind, including all thoughts and feelings. You may be stuck in traffic and getting anxious. Ask yourself, 'What's happening to me right at this moment?' Make a note of what you notice.

   ✔ **Accept:** Acknowledge that this particular moment in time is your present-moment experience. Trying to force yourself to think or feel something else isn't going to stop your anxiety from existing in the here and now. Remember that acceptance isn't giving up, though, and it doesn't mean that this situation will be this way forever. It just means accepting the moment as it is, right now.

✔ **Investigate with kindness:** Become aware of emotions in your body. Notice whereabouts you feel them. These sensations can be challenging, so bring as much of a sense of warmth and kindness as you can. (See Chapter 6 for more on kindness and compassion toward yourself).

✔ **Nonidentify:** Step back and get a wider perspective on your experience; watch as it unfolds instead of becoming it.

For example, you can get a sense of anxiety, rather than being anxious, as you watch your anxious thoughts and emotions from a wider perspective. Imagine watching your experience as you would a movie at the cinema.

The acronym *RAIN* was first coined about 20 years ago by Michele McDonald. For more on stepping back, check out the later section 'Trying different mindful metaphors' for ideas to help you step back.

Considering the effect of mindful attention on your thoughts

The more mindful attention you place on your thoughts, the less scary or threatening they become. Bringing attitudes such as curiosity, acceptance, awareness and nonjudgement towards your thoughts can be very helpful. All these attitudes come under the umbrella of *mindful attention.*

Without mindfulness, you can feel stuck or trapped by your anxious thoughts as you self-identify with them and want to block them out or stop them. Mindful attention gives you a different perspective and a sense of freedom from the trap of anxious thoughts and feelings.

Here are some of the negative, unhelpful responses you may have when you don't bring mindful attention to your thoughts:

✔ I can't calm down. I hate feeling like this.

✔ I can't get rid of these horrible anxious feelings.

✔ I'm always stressed, and I feel so tense. I can never relax.

When you start to practise mindful attention toward your thoughts, your responses change along the following lines:

- ✔ I'm aware of the tension that I get in my jaw. I'm curious about it, but I don't self-identify with it. It's just a feeling.

- ✔ I'm having stressful thoughts, but I'm watching them rather than feeling part of them. They're going to pass.

- ✔ I notice the anxiety in my body and mind, and I accept it, just as it is.

Trying different mindful metaphors

Sometimes, getting a sense of stepping back or decentring from your thoughts is difficult. Here are some suggestions and mindful imagery to help you:

- ✔ Imagine leaves floating down a stream and you placing your thoughts on them for a few minutes, watching from the side of the bank.

- ✔ Picture yourself on a train and watching the scenery go past. Place your thoughts on the scenery.

- ✔ Visualise bubbles floating through the air and imagine your thoughts inside those bubbles, watching them float away.

- ✔ Practise the clouds and mountain meditation in Chapter 5.

Understanding That Thoughts Aren't Necessarily Facts

Not every thought you have is a fact. Often thoughts are just a selection of pictures and words that arise in your consciousness. If you don't have an awareness of what you're thinking, however, you may think all kinds of limiting and self-critical thoughts without even realizing it. These are called *automatic thoughts*.

For example, you may have left the oven turned up too high and overcooked your dinner, or you may have forgotten to pick up an item from the supermarket. Thoughts can then arise such as 'I'm so useless' or 'I can't do anything right'. But these acts are simple mistakes that lots of people make. Plus, you may not even be aware that you're having these kinds of thoughts in response to the situation. These thoughts can build up over time and impact your mood and the way you see yourself.

Discovering that thoughts are just thoughts

Imagine this scenario: You've had work friends over for dinner. The next day, one of your colleagues doesn't come in for work, and you find out that he isn't very well. What first thoughts spring to mind for you? Are they things like 'I've poisoned my friend', 'I feel so bad I made my friend sick' or 'No one will ever want to come over again'?

Now think carefully about the facts of the scenario. The only thing you know for sure is that your friend is sick: That's the fact. The rest is just a succession of spiralling thoughts created by your mind.

Can you see how your mind is quick to jump to conclusions with little evidence? You probably had these negative thoughts before your mind stopped to consider that your friend may have the flu and other people at your dinner party are absolutely fine. Your homemade vegetable lasagna wasn't to blame at all!

Identifying yourself as separate from your thoughts

If you stare really closely at the pages of a book so that your nose is nearly touching it, the pages are a dark blur, and you can't make out individual words or pictures. You certainly can't read or understand what the book is about.

But when you gradually move the book slowly away from your face, you're able to make out words, shapes, pictures, sentences and paragraphs. As you move it even farther away from your face, you can also notice what's around the book — say, your desk and other furniture and decor in your home or workplace.

Similarly, when you're so close to your thoughts that you notice only them, you don't have a wider perspective. You may be having unhelpful thoughts that you identify with because you're unable to see the wider picture. Stepping back from your thoughts allows you to distance yourself from them and therefore lose your self-identity with them. Doing so gives you a greater sense of control and choice and allows you to make wiser decisions.

For example, sometimes I sit down to write, and I get stuck. I give myself a time limit in which to continue trying to force myself to write. When I exceed the time limit and am still struggling to get words on the page, I take a step back. I have a break, maybe some food and begin again later on or even the next day. By taking this step back, I allow myself to return to my work refreshed instead of becoming frustrated as I sit and struggle to work. You can do the same when you step back from your thoughts.

Accepting your thoughts with nonjudgemental awareness

Having uncomfortable thoughts that you're trying to accept can be challenging. Therefore, bringing a nonjudgemental attitude is vital to allow other attitudes to emerge, such as curiosity and acceptance. Instead of labelling a thought as inherently bad or good, try to allow it just to be there.

For example, you may have a thought such as 'I'm useless at this' or 'No one here likes me'. Instead of judging those thoughts as bad or something that you shouldn't feel or think, bring a sense of curiosity, kindness and acceptance to that thought instead.

All thoughts are just that: thoughts.

Dealing with unhelpful or disturbing thoughts

When you practise mindfulness, you become more aware of your body and your mind, including your thoughts. If you're suffering from anxiety, you may have tried hard to ignore these thoughts, suppress them or run away from them. As your awareness becomes much greater, some difficult or disturbing thoughts may arise for you and feel much more intense than they did before.

Here's an action plan to manage these difficult thoughts with mindfulness:

1. **Take a step back.**

   You can do so in several ways:

   • Use one of the metaphors in the earlier 'Trying different mindful metaphors' section to place your thoughts on.

   • Label the thoughts. What type of thought are you having? Are you worrying, planning, judging or being self-critical?

   • Notice the thought you're having and ask yourself whether it's a thought or a fact.

   • Make a note of the thoughts that you're having. Sometimes writing them down can feel like a release.

Try each of these different methods and find the one that generally works best for you. Remember that this isn't an exercise in avoidance.

2. **Go back to what you were doing at the moment the difficult thought(s) arose.**

   If you were meditating, turn your attention back to focusing on your breath. If you were at work, commuting or having a meal, turn your attention back to your senses then. So, for example, you can rest your attention on the sounds at work or the touch of your fingers on the keyboard or the smells of different food being cooked.

You can also use mindful walking as you simply walk from room to room or building to building. You can slow your pace down a bit and put your awareness on your feet as you walk on the solid ground. Be mindful of your breath as you are walking. This unites the body and mind.

If you're finding your thoughts incredibly hard to deal with and they're extremely upsetting, disturbing or harmful to yourself or others, contact a medical professional before you continue with any of these exercises.

Discovering the Breathing Space Meditation

The breathing space meditation is a short one that you can practise for three minutes or more a day, so you can fit it around your daily life. It's useful whenever you need to take a step back, want a change in perception or have to deal with a stressful or upsetting event.

The three aspects of the breathing-space meditation are memorable with ABC:

- ✔ **Awareness** of bodily sensations
- ✔ Focusing on the **Breath**
- ✔ **Consciously** expanding your awareness

Practising the breathing space meditation

Find a comfortable sitting position on a chair or the floor. Sit with your back straight and away from the back of the chair if you can (this sends a signal to your brain that you're alert). Of course, you don't have to sit. You can lie down or stand, whichever is most comfortable and appropriate at that moment.

When you're comfortable, follow these steps:

1. **Become aware of yourself.**

    Ask yourself the following questions:

    - 'What sensations in the body am I feeling right now?' Become aware of all sensations, even if they're very uncomfortable, such as aches and pains. Accept the discomfort as much as possible.

    - 'What thoughts am I aware of at this moment, passing through my mind?' Become aware of your thoughts and the space between you and your thoughts. Observe the thoughts without becoming caught up in them.

2. **Focus your attention on your breathing.**

    Feel the breath wherever it's easiest for you, whether that's the back of the throat, the nose, the mouth, the chest or the tummy area. Feel the whole of each in-breath and the whole of each out-breath. Just become aware of the breath instead of trying to change it and force it to become a certain way. Be curious, warm and friendly toward it. Does each breath feel a little different to you? Be grateful for your breathing that's keeping you alive and well.

3. **Expand your awareness to your whole body.**

    Imagine the entire body is breathing. See whether you can feel the effect of where the energy is settling.

4. **Accept yourself as whole, perfect and complete just in this moment.**

    Try to bring as much of an acceptance toward yourself and the practice as you can. Be aware of any judgments you may make without reacting to them automatically. Bring as much kindness to yourself as possible.

Finding out the benefits and use of the breathing space meditation

The breathing space meditation has loads of benefits, including making you more self-aware and pulling you into the present moment. It also helps you become an observer of your experience instead of feeling trapped or pulled along by it. This realisation helps when anxious feelings arise, allowing you to take a step back from them instead of letting them consume you.

This stepping back also allows you to see things from a different perspective and gives space for new ideas and creativity to form and expand.

Discovering when to practise the breathing space meditation

The breathing space meditation is very short, so you can practise it almost anywhere. I suggest about three times a day for three minutes each. You can also practise it as the *coping breathing space* when a specific stressful, upsetting or frustrating situation arises.

You practise the coping breathing space exactly the same as the breathing space meditation, except that you use it at the moment anxiety is rising up for you instead of at the regularly scheduled time. It helps you tune into being mindful of the anxiety rather than avoiding it, running away from it or being overwhelmed by it.

For example, say that you've had an uncomfortable disagreement with a work colleague or a family member, or you've recalled an unpleasant event from your past. The coping breathing space is like taking a break, and it allows you to better handle the difficult feelings you're experiencing.

Whenever you use it, the breathing-space meditation isn't about running away from your problems, emotions or feelings. Instead, it's about moving toward them with a sense of curiosity and warmth. Doing so isn't easy, but even if you can manage it in tiny amounts, you've made a huge step.

Chapter 5

Practising Deeper Mindfulness Meditations for Anxiety

. . . .

In This Chapter

▶ Discovering the body scan meditation

▶ Practising a sitting meditation

▶ Overcoming anxiety with mindful imagery

. . . .

*Y*ou may not be familiar with the concept of being in the present moment and being aware of yourself and your body in the present moment. In modern society and everyday living, you can all too easily become disconnected from yourself, tending to live in your head which is lost in thoughts, future plans and worries. This chapter is about reconnecting with yourself using your mind, body and breath.

I describe three different styles of meditation: one focused mainly on the body; another focused on increasing your whole awareness; and the third focused on increasing attention to your thoughts and emotions. All three styles of meditation overlap in the sense that they incorporate all the three elements, but getting to know a range of different techniques is helpful, as is discovering what you find easiest or most comfortable when practising mindfulness.

 Each meditation has different benefits for managing anxiety, but I suggest that you do them in the order I set them out in this chapter because they gently help increase your awareness step by step.

Introducing the Body Scan Meditation

Have you ever noticed a tendency to live in your head? Most people do on a day-to-day basis, without ever connecting with their body. Some people refer to it as the "talking head". They think of their body as just a structure that serves to carry the brain around! They don't take much notice of the rest of the body, unless they feel pain, are hungry or need to use the bathroom!

Getting into this unhelpful mental state is easy. Factors such as too much paperwork, a stressful job and a busy lifestyle can all contribute to this disconnection from your body. In fact, multitasking is the ultimate factor in becoming disconnected from the body, something that modern society doesn't help with by emphasising how you can better multitask with all the available gadgets!

You can correct this disconnection from the body with simple exercises, such as the body scan. The body scan helps you reconnect mindfully with your body by using kind, nonjudgemental, nonstriving, gentle attention on the body itself. You do so by kindly focusing your mindful awareness on zones of the body bit by bit, perhaps together with your breathing.

Discovering the benefits and purpose of the body scan

Ever tried breathing through your toes? Sounds a bit odd, I know, but in fact this is one of the ways that you can use to guide your breath and mindful attention through your body!

The body scan has many benefits:

> ✔ **Tuning into bodily sensations:** The body scan helps you be more aware of your bodily sensations and therefore more aware of anxiety as it arises in your body. Being able to catch your anxiety feelings early as they arise puts you in a position where you can regain some of your control over your anxiety before negative thoughts and emotions spiral away from your reach.

✔ **Tuning the mind into the present moment:** Instead of getting lost in worrying thoughts and being stressed or anxious about events in the future, you focus on the present moment. Your body is ever-present. As you focus on different parts of the body while doing the scan, you ground your focus into what's happening now, which is a body scan.

✔ **Allowing and accepting emotions instead of suppressing them:** Stressful events from your past, such as a divorce, job loss or the loss of a loved one, can cause great fear and can get locked in your body as physical tension. With the body scan, you bring emotions to the surface and release them, allowing then to express themselves. Think of how a flower slowly opens itself to reveal its petals and then withers and dies over time. Your emotions are much the same. If you suppress them, they're remain always just below the surface, ready to burst through. But if you allow them to flower, they go through their natural lifecycle and slowly wither away.

Practising the body scan

The body scan is about getting back in touch with your body. It's a time totally for yourself. Find a comfortable place where you won't be disturbed for 10 to 30 minutes depending on how long you decide to practise for.

The body scan is about accepting yourself as you are, not pushing to improve yourself, so try allowing whatever happens to just happen.

You may find it relaxing, but the aim of this practice isn't just to try to relax. In fact, your experience of the body scan may well be different every time, so don't worry about trying to find a right or wrong way to practise. Instead, the body scan is about simply allowing your experience to be, just as it is.

Sometimes, practising the body scan is easier when you listen to a guided meditation. Have a search for some at www.youtube.com using the keywords 'guided body scan meditation', go to my website (www.joellemarshall.com) or listen to the audio that accompanies *Mindfulness Workbook For Dummies* by Shamash Alidina and myself (Wiley). (Use Track 2 at www.dummies.com/go/mindfulnessworkbookuk.)

Allow yourself 10 to 30 minutes for the following meditation or whatever feels right for you. Wear comfortable clothes and loosen any tight clothing.

1. **Lie down in a comfortable, warm position on a yoga mat, for example, or a bed.**

   You can cover yourself with a blanket if you think you're likely to feel cold later in the practice.

2. **Place your palms facing upward, hands down by your sides and legs slightly apart.**

   Close your eyes.

3. **Be aware of your attitude.**

   Decide that you're going to allow and accept whatever arises in this meditation as best you can.

4. **Notice the weight of your body on the floor, mat or bed.**

   Feel the contact of your whole body with the ground from your head to your heels.

5. **Focus on your breathing for a few minutes.**

   Don't force your breathing to be a certain way; just try to notice it as it is.

6. **Take a deep breath and imagine it going down your body, down your chest, abdomen and pelvis into your left leg, all the way down until it reaches the big toe of your left foot.**

   If imagining your breath going down your body doesn't work for you, you don't have to do it.

7. **Focus on the big toe of your left foot, bringing a sense of curiosity to the sensations.**

   Does it feel cold or warm? Can you feel any contact of, say, the socks with your toe?

8. **Expand your awareness to your little toe and all the toes in between.**

   What does the sensation feel like? If you can't feel anything, just be aware of the lack of sensation.

9. **Expand your awareness to the sole of your left foot.**

   Focus on the heel and ball of the foot. What do they feel like? Again, if you don't feel anything, just be aware of the lack of sensation.

10. **Repeat this process slowly, moving up the leg, the ankle, the kneecap, the thigh and the hip.**

    Bring curiosity to each body part, again being aware of any sensations or lack of sensations. Breathe deeply and imagine the breath going all the way down the body into the part you're focusing on. Does your left leg now feel different to the right?

11. **Shift your attention gently to your right leg, imagining the breath going all the way down into the big toe of the right foot.**

    Repeat the process you did with the left leg in Steps 7 to 10.

12. **Focus your awareness on the pelvic region, including your hips and bottom.**

    Breathe into them and imagine you're filling them with nourishing oxygen. If doing so helps, visualise your pelvic region as a bowl situated in between your hips and focus on filling it with your breath.

13. **Move your attention upwards gently toward your lower abdomen and lower back; notice the movement as you breathe in and out.**

    This area is where emotions can get stored in the body. Without judgement, see whether you can accept whatever arises. If you feel anxiety or some other emotion, see whether you can just accept the experience as it is. If that's too overwhelming, you can always come back to your breathing or the feeling in your feet.

14. **Move your attention and awareness gently to your chest and upper back.**

    Feel your ribcage rising and falling. Be aware of any emotions rising from the heart area. Again, just allow them to be present without judgement.

15. **Concentrate on the fingertips of both hands together.**

    Imagine the breath moving upwards through both arms, past the elbows and into the shoulders.

16. **Move your mindful attention from your neck to your jaw, being aware of any tension there, move it onto the face, becoming aware of any frowning on the forehead, and then finally move your attention to the top of your head.**

    Bring a sense of gratitude for your brain and all the amazing abilities that are located in the head, such as your vision, your hearing and your sense of smell.

17. **Imagine a space at the top of the head and a space at the bottom of the feet, if you feel comfortable doing so; take a deep breath and imagine that the breath is going from the top of the head sweeping down the body, down both arms, down the chest, the abdomen, the pelvis and down both legs.**

    Imagine that breath is filling you with energy and life-saving oxygen.

18. **Let go of any efforts you've been making to practise mindfulness and get a sense of your body as a whole.**

    Rest with the knowledge that you're whole, perfect and complete just as you are.

The body scan is generally a safe exercise to do. However, if you've had a stressful event in your past, you may have suppressed feelings about it. The body scan may unlock painful emotions that have been stored in your body over time. If you find this very difficult to cope with, try seeking advice from a qualified therapist or mindfulness teacher. If you can, though, open up to these feelings and sensations and see what happens. You may find that they start to dissolve in their own time.

Overcoming common difficulties that arise with the body scan

The body scan may be an unusual concept for you, particularly if you haven't been in touch with your body for a while. The following difficulties are common and nothing to worry about, especially if you've had an unusual experience with the body scan:

✔ **You fall asleep.** People tend to lead busy lives, and maybe the body scan is the first time you've had to lie down and do nothing in some time. Make sure that you're getting enough sleep and try practising at another time of the day if you find that helpful. If you still keep falling asleep, don't be too hard on yourself. Try a different position, such as sitting up with your back supported. The main thing is to keep practising whether you fall asleep or not.

✔ **You can't feel any sensation.** Don't worry if you can't feel sensation in certain parts or large areas of the body. Mindfulness is about accepting the lack of sensation just as much as accepting any sensations that may arise. With more practice over time, you may start to feel more physical sensation. If not, it doesn't matter.

✔ **You feel more anxious or stressed.** From picking up a book about managing anxiety with mindfulness, the last thing you probably want is for your anxious feelings to be exacerbated.

Mindfulness isn't relaxation, and you may feel worse before you feel better. If you're trying to achieve a certain experience, let that idea go. If the anxiety keeps coming, explore the feeling of it within your body. Bring your attention to where you feel the sensation specifically and gently allow it to rest there. Try not to be critical with yourself.

✔ **You feel bored or restless.** If you're used to rushing around, being active and never staying still, you may find the body scan boring and begin to feel restless.

Instead of giving up, try to become aware of the feelings of boredom or restlessness within your body. Bring a sense of curiosity to the feelings. What do they feel like? What colour or shape are they? Becoming aware of these feelings and lack of concentration is the essence of mindfulness. The boredom or restlessness should disappear in time.

✔ **You feel difficult or disturbing emotions.** Sometimes the practice of the body scan can release suppressed emotions. As you relax into the body scan, thoughts and emotions can arise into your conscious awareness and then be released. Try and accept the feelings as they come, just as they are.

✔ **You feel a bit dizzy.** Open your eyes for a few minutes, come out of the practice and allow your mind to settle. When you're ready, start again, with your eyes open if it helps you ground yourself.

✔ **You feel like you want to move.** If you're not used to it, lying down in one position for a period of time can begin to feel quite uncomfortable. If you feel the urge to move while practising the body scan try, do so in a mindful way. Move slowly and with awareness on the parts of the body you're moving. Try to make yourself more comfortable at the beginning of the practice by using more pillows under your knees or wherever you need.

Introducing the Sitting Meditation

The sitting meditation is simply about being mindful but in a seated position.

Practise this meditation after a couple of weeks of daily body scan practice (see the earlier 'Introducing the Body Scan Meditation' section).

Discovering the purpose and benefits of the sitting meditation

Sitting meditation follows on from the body scan's focus on bringing your attention back to your breath and body. But it increases your attention even further, by increasing a wider range of present-moment experiences to be aware of. Your mind still strays into different thoughts, as is perfectly natural, but you begin to change your relationship towards your thoughts.

If you have anxiety and perhaps anxious thoughts that you aren't even usually aware of, the sitting meditation may be able to change your relationship with these thoughts. As a result, instead of identifying with them, you can take a step back and just observe them.

Also, mindfulness of breath, the first section of the sitting meditation, can help engage the relaxation response. This process can increase your ability to focus, thus allowing you to place your attention on something other than your anxious thoughts or feelings.

The sitting meditation comprises several stages and breaks up thoughts, feelings and bodily sensations. This arrangement allows you more easily to pinpoint and manage your anxiety wherever it arises, whether in thoughts, feelings or bodily sensations.

Practising the sitting meditation

Sitting meditation is also called the *expanding awareness meditation* and has been used for thousands of years. You can choose from different seated postures. Select one of the following positions that's most comfortable and right for you when you practise:

✔ **Sitting on a chair:** People generally tend to slouch in chairs, including at the office. For meditation, sit up away from the back of the chair and support your own weight with a straight back and spine, if you can. Already this sends a signal to your brain that you're alert and something different is happening.

Try putting magazines or something similar under the back two legs of the chair because it tilts you slightly forward and helps your back to straighten naturally. Place your feet flat on the floor, put your hands face down on your knees or place them in each other. Allow your head to lift naturally and gently until it's 'balanced' on your head and shoulders and then lean forward and backward a few times until you find the right position for you.

✔ **Sitting on the floor:** You may have seen the *Burmese position* before among experienced meditators or Buddhist monks: the cross-legged position on top of a cushion or blanket on a soft ground. To adopt this position, stretch out your legs and any other part of the body that needs a stretch. Cross your legs and allow the knees to touch the ground. If they don't touch the ground, use more cushions to support the knees.

Allow the heel of the left foot to touch gently the inside of the right thigh. Your right leg should be in front of the left leg with the heel pointing toward the lower left leg. If you find this difficult, adjust yourself as much as you can until you're comfortable. Lean forward and backward until you feel like you're in a comfortable position and your head feels balanced on your shoulders and neck.

When you find a seated position with which you feel comfortable, begin the stages of sitting meditation. If you want to begin with just one stage at a time, that's perfectly okay. But you can also do all the stages from the start if you feel comfortable enough.

Do this practice for about 30 minutes, spending 5 to 6 minutes on each section, but you can do less or more if you feel like it.

1. **Be mindful of your breath.**

   Sit in a chair or on the floor. Gently become aware of your breathing. Try to sense the breath where it feels easiest: perhaps the nose or back of the throat, the chest or the abdomen.

   Don't force the breath to be a certain way; just gently notice it, with a sense of warmth and kindness. Your mind wandering off to other thoughts is perfectly natural. Just gently guide it back to the focus of the breath.

2. **Be mindful of your body.**

   Gently expand your awareness to your whole body. Become aware of any bodily sensations. If you have aches and pains, try to bring a sense of acceptance to them as best you can. Imagine your breath going in and out of that part of the body.

3. **Be mindful of sounds.**

   Gently open your awareness to any sounds you can hear. Try to notice how your mind labels a sound and can bring judgements to it.

   For example, I'm sitting in the library at this moment, and I opened my awareness to sounds. I can hear the traffic going past. My mind automatically thinks it's a bad sound, and the library windows should be shut. But I was able to bring awareness to my mind's judgements and think of the sounds as neutral and not an annoyance.

Become aware of the volume, pitch and quality of the sounds as they change from moment to moment. Notice the silence between and underneath all sounds. Let the sounds come to you instead of reaching for them. Then gently rest your attention on the sounds.

4. Be mindful of thoughts.

Become aware of your thoughts, but try not to become caught up in them; just be an observer of your thoughts. Remember that your thoughts aren't facts but merely thoughts (see Chapter 4 for more). Watch the thoughts arise and pass away, just like sounds do.

5. Be open in awareness.

Just notice whatever you're most aware of – your thoughts, your bodily sensations, the sounds you can hear or your breath, whichever is strongest for you at this time. Have a choiceless awareness, which means stay open to everything that happens in your present moment experience without preference. If your mind wanders off or gets pulled along in a train of thought, just gently guide it back to the breath and begin again. Bring a sense of patience and curiosity throughout this practice if you can.

Overcoming difficulties with the sitting meditation

You may encounter some common difficulties with the sitting meditation, many of which overlap with those of the body scan. Check out 'Overcoming common difficulties that arise with the body scan' earlier in this chapter and see whether you spot similarities with the difficulties you may be facing with the sitting meditation – such as your mind wandering off or falling asleep.

Here are a couple of extra difficulties that you may find with the sitting meditation:

⮑ **Discomfort merely from sitting for that length of time:** A very common problem, especially with people who aren't used to sitting and meditating. If you do a job where you crouch over a desk all day, your muscles aren't accustomed to sitting up straight in this position.

Stand up, mindfully stretching out a bit, and then return to sitting.

✔ **Constant discomfort or pain when practising:** If you feel pain or discomfort, try to move your attention toward it instead of trying to push it away or ignore it. Bring a sense of acceptance to it if you can, while also being aware of your breathing. Try to relax into acceptance of the pain or discomfort, which may sound odd, but bring as much relaxation and acceptance as you can.

If it is severely uncomfortable for you to sit in a cross-legged position for a long time and causes unnecessary pain, then, of course, you don't have to practise it like that. Try another seated position, such as sitting upright on a chair. You can also lie down for this meditation if you want. Be aware of what is right for you – this meditation can be practiced either sitting or lying down.

Discovering Mindful Imagery Meditations for Anxiety

Sometimes doing mindful imagery can help when you're practising mindfulness: it can make things clearer for you. The two mindful imagery meditations in this section help you step away from identifying yourself with your thoughts and cope better with whatever's coming your way.

When you separate your thoughts from your identification with them, negative thoughts have no room to expand and increase your anxiety. These meditations allow you to picture how you can separate yourself and also become a grounded observer, while your thoughts arrive and pass away.

Mindful imagery isn't a form of escapism. It's about being as present as possible in order to picture the setting as fully as you can. Imagine being present and connecting with your senses within your imagination as best you can.

Practising the clouds in the sky visual meditation

This visualisation helps aid you in the mindfulness tool of seeing your thoughts as separate from yourself:

1. **Lie down in a comfortable position and gently close your eyes.**

2. **Imagine that it's a warm, sunny day and you're lying on soft grass at the side of a lake, on a beach or in a park, whichever feels most relaxed for you.**

3. **Look up at the beautiful blue sky and watch some clouds passing.**

4. **Move your awareness gently to your thoughts and when you become aware of a thought, place it on a cloud and watch it pass by.**

5. **Continue this process for a few minutes, whenever you become aware of a thought.**

This meditation is easy to do at any time and is particularly useful when you're feeling very anxious. Also, try it at night before sleep, if you find that your mind tends to race.

Standing tall with the mountain meditation

The mountain meditation helps you deal with strong emotions and whatever arises for you. It's a way of visualising yourself as a whole complete being, while everything else rises and eventually falls away – another important tool of mindfulness.

To practise the mountain meditation, carry out these steps:

1. **Sit upright and take a couple of deep breaths.**

   As you breathe in, imagine your breath giving you energy and vitality. As you breathe out, imagine a sense of letting go.

2. **Let your breath return to normal.**

   Gently close your eyes.

3. **Visualise a beautiful, majestic mountain, standing high above the rest of the landscape.**

   The mountain is strong and sturdy, unaffected by the rain, wind and snow that it faces. Imagine watching the mountain go through every season and encountering sunshine, storms and blizzards. Notice how the mountain is unaffected by everything going on around it.

4. **Imagine yourself as this mountain – strong, stable, balanced and grounded.**

   You're ever-present, despite what your thoughts and emotions are doing. They change like the seasons, but the essence of your being is still the same whatever arises for you, just like the mountain.

If you're struggling to visualise, don't worry; some people are more visual than others. In fact, I know mindfulness teachers who aren't very visual! If you can't conjure up any images for your visualisations and are struggling, just concentrate on the other meditations in this chapter.

Savouring the Mindful Eating Meditation

The mindful eating meditation is a simple one to get you from becoming lost in your thoughts back to the present moment.

Have you ever walked into a room and thought 'What did I come in here for?' That's called being on *automatic pilot* or the *doing mode.* Your mind isn't on the task at hand and has wandered off from the present moment. Though not necessarily bad some of the time, if you're constantly on automatic pilot, you may not be aware of any anxious or negative thoughts you're having. You're missing out on your life now because you're not living in the present, and you may be getting into bad habits without even realising.

Practising mindful eating

You can carry out the mindful eating meditation with any small piece of food, such as a raisin, a cranberry, a chocolate bar or a small piece of fruit, such as an apple.

Allow yourself about ten minutes for this meditation, longer if you can. It's an easy meditation to do anywhere, out and about or at work. All you need is a small piece of food that you can hold in one hand – so best avoid soup!

Get a pen and paper and note down your experience: write down everything you experience if you want to. Making a note of it can help you to notice any differences with your experiences of food before and after this meditation.

Here's how to practise the mindful eating meditation:

1. **Get the piece of food and place it before you.**

   What do you notice about its appearance? What colour is it? What shape is it? If appropriate, what's the skin like? Look closely and be as specific as possible.

2. **Pick up the piece of food and roll it in your hand.**

   What does the texture feel like against your skin? Close your eyes to help you get a real sense of the feeling in your hand. Is it heavy? Is it light? Does it feel hollow? Does it feel full? Gently squeeze it and see how it feels.

3. **Hold the piece of food close to your ear, rolling it in your hand gently as you do so.**

   Can you hear any sounds within the food? If you can't hear anything, what does the silence feel like?

4. **Move the food towards your nose.**

   What does it smell like? Try to mindfully feel the sensations in your arm as you move it. If you can smell the food, does the smell bring up any memories for you?

5. **Bring the food towards your mouth.**

   Notice whether your mouth is watering. Touch the food to your lips and be aware of any sensations there. Take a bite. Do you notice any sound? If so, what does it sound like? Move the piece of food around your mouth feeling the weight of it. Note the taste of it as it releases its juices and you gently start to chew. Feel the sensation of your teeth as you chew.

Reflect on the experience of the food meditation. Did the food taste any different? Was it different to your normal experience of eating that piece of food?

If you didn't feel anything different, don't worry; just be aware of the lack of sensation you had when practising the mindful eating meditation. You may be used to eating when watching TV, at your desk working or on the run, so this exercise may be quite unusual for you. Try experimenting with different foods and notice your thoughts compared to foods you like or dislike.

Make your way over to Chapter 8 for more on fitting mindful eating into your everyday life. Also, don't forget to check out my mindful cooking practice in Chapter 11.

Chapter 6

Using Mindful Self-Compassion and Kindness for Anxiety

- -

In This Chapter

▶ Discovering how to practise loving-kindness

▶ Reducing the need for perfectionism

▶ Understanding how self-compassion is helpful

- -

*T*his chapter is about being kinder to yourself in a mindful way. When anxious, you're more likely to think negatively and berate yourself — for example, for not being perfect (despite the fact that no one is!).

The practices I describe – such as the loving-kindness meditations that are proved to reduce anxiety – can help you counteract this tendency, and lead to higher levels of well-being. And don't worry that this self-compassion is going to turn you into an egotistical monster because I also describe the importance of directing compassion to other people as well.

Understanding Loving-Kindness

Loving-kindness is basically the idea of evoking love toward every human being on the planet, including yourself.

The practice of loving-kindness helps generate a sense of friendliness toward yourself and others.

Generally, you achieve this sense of friendliness through practising loving-kindness meditations, which traditionally can be up to 45 minutes long. But in this section, I offer you a range of loving-kindness practices, directed to yourself and others, that vary in time. This flexibility makes practising loving-kindness much easier in today's busy world.

Accepting the importance of being kind to yourself

You may not realise that you're irrationally hard on yourself on a day-to-day basis. For example, perhaps you get to work and notice that you've forgotten your lunch or that you've double-booked something in your diary by accident. In such cases, negative thoughts can arise such as 'I'm such an idiot for forgetting' or 'I can't believe I did that!'.

But these kinds of situation happen to everybody. You need to be kind to yourself and realise that everyone makes mistakes from time to time, and that's just part of life. However, if you become used to berating yourself every time you make a mistake (and this self-criticism can be a pattern you learnt from childhood), bringing yourself out of it can be difficult.

One of the best and most helpful suggestions I ever received about self-kindness was to think of myself as a young child — not when I personally was young, but a small child in general of around 6 years of age. I was advised to treat myself as I would that young child. I found that thinking of this child as separate from myself and treating myself accordingly very helpful. For example, I made sure that I got enough sleep, ate healthily and was generally a lot kinder to myself.

Practising loving-kindness for yourself

Loving-kindness meditation is often called *metta* or compassion meditation. I recommend doing this meditation after you've had some practice of other meditations, such as the body scan or the sitting meditations (check out Chapter 5).

This loving-kindness meditation varies slightly from other meditations in that it's quite visual and promotes positive emotions, such as well-wishing or compassion toward yourself.

Before you start, get into a comfortable sitting position. Allow 10 to 15 minutes and make sure that you won't be disturbed. Turn off the TV, computer and mobile phone and find a quiet place. If you can, do something relaxing beforehand, such as having a warm bath or a cup of tea. Wrap yourself in a blanket and make sure that you're warm and cosy!

1. **Breathe mindfully with a sense of gratitude.**

   Begin by focusing on your natural breathing. Simply rest your awareness on your breath and be thankful that your breath is keeping you alive. Feel the same sense of gratitude and thankfulness that your breath is nourishing your body with oxygen.

2. **Well-wish towards yourself.**

   Visualise yourself and wish yourself a sense of well-being. Say to yourself, several times, 'May I be well, may I be happy, may I be healthy, may I be free from suffering'.

3. **Feel the words radiating out from your heart.**

   Don't force any feelings. Even if you don't feel any positive emotion, that's perfectly fine.

This meditation may feel difficult for you, especially at the beginning of your mindfulness journey. People commonly struggle with this exercise. If challenging emotions come up for you, try practising loving-kindness to someone else you find easy to love or even a pet. Then come back to this exercise in the future.

Your mind is bound to wander to other thoughts. Bring a spirit of kindness to your practice, especially in this meditation.

Well-wishing loving-kindness for others

Practising loving-kindness for others is important because it helps give you a sense of warmth and well-wishing to their welfare, which in turn raises your own well-being level. Even if you don't have many positive feelings toward a person to begin with, loving-kindness helps you let go of those aggravations, which in turn makes you feel better.

As with practising loving-kindness towards yourself (see the preceding section), get into a comfortable position and try to do something relaxing beforehand. Allow 15 to 20 minutes for this meditation.

People normally practise loving-kindness by offering kindness to themselves first and then to others. If you feel like you're ready to do this meditation, allow yourself 20 minutes and incorporate loving-kindness for yourself before you move onto others. If you feel this meditation is too difficult for you to do the whole 20 minutes to start with, do the meditation as I set it out, in two parts.

1. **Start with some mindful breathing.**

   Focus on your breath with a sense of gratitude.

2. **Well-wish towards someone you find easy to show affection for.**

   Choose someone with whom you have a simple uncomplicated relationship, such as a close friend, a relative such as an aunt or uncle, a spiritual or wise person that you know or even a pet.

   I suggest not choosing a partner because that's a more complex relationship.

   Visualise this person and, in your mind, say to yourself several times, slowly and thoughtfully, 'May you be well, may you be happy, may you be healthy, may you be free from suffering'.

   Say it with a sense of kindness and affection. You don't need to force any specific emotion to arise.

3. Well-wish toward someone neutral.

Think of someone for whom you have neither positive nor negative feelings, such as a local shopkeeper you see every day or the people who do your dry cleaning. You can even think of someone who commutes on the same train to work as you but you've never spoken to.

Say 'May you be well, may you be happy, may you be healthy, may you be free from suffering'.

Visualise and wish the person well, as best as you can.

4. Well-wish towards someone difficult.

This step is sometimes not the easiest! Think of someone who you don't particularly like — perhaps someone who annoys or irritates you. Choose someone you have a difficult relationship with but feel willing to work with today.

Visualise the person and say, 'May you be well, may you be happy, may you be healthy, may you be free from suffering'.

You're not condoning what the person has done; you're simply wishing them well and not holding a grudge. This person won't know that you're doing this meditation, but you may feel a huge weight lift off your shoulders as you let go of some of your negative feelings.

5. Well-wish towards your loved person, your neutral person and your difficult person.

Imagine all three of them together. See whether you can wish everyone a sense of equal well-being. After all, they're human beings deserving of happiness.

6. Well-wish to everyone on the planet.

Wish everyone on the planet, including all sentient beings, such as animals, a sense of wellbeing. Imagine coming out of your front door and the street you live in, wishing everyone there happiness. Then zoom out to the area you live in, followed by the town or city, the country, the continent and the earth as a whole.

Think of all the people in the world: the children, the families, the retired. Think of all the lakes, rivers, seas and mountains. Think of all the animals that exist on the planet.

Wish them all a sense of happiness and wellness. Use the words 'May they all be well, may they all be happy, may they all be healthy, may they all be free from suffering'.

Facing common issues with the loving-kindness meditation

Some common difficulties may arise for you with loving-kindness meditation:

- ✔ **You can't feel any kind or compassionate feelings towards another person.** That's okay; just try to wish a sense of kindness, even if you don't feel it.

- ✔ **You find that the meditation makes you feel worse.** In fact, this feeling may be a good thing for you because you're releasing stored emotions and letting them go. Still, if you find the meditation too upsetting, take a break, talk to someone you trust and come back to it when you feel a bit stronger.

- ✔ **You can't feel any affection towards yourself.** This experience is normal. People are often taught the importance of looking after others but not necessarily themselves. Take your time with it and practise after a body scan or a sitting meditation if you find that helpful. (I describe these meditations in Chapter 5.)

Letting Go of the Perfectionist

Perfectionism goes hand in hand with anxiety. Perfectionists tend to be high achievers trying to do their very best at everything. They seldom enjoy what they do because they're too busy striving for perfection. They never live in the present moment and make their happiness dependent in their achievements.

Investigating what being a perfectionist really means

Anxiety comes about because perfectionists aim for perfection and yet never quite achieve it. They think that they have to have the perfect job, the perfect partner, the perfect house, the perfect group of friends or the perfect body. But they can't meet these extremely high (often impossible) expectations, which causes anxiety. Thoughts occur, such as 'I must do this right', 'I mustn't fail', 'I must get everything done' and 'Everyone must like me'. They need their life to look a certain way in order to be happy, but this ideal is always just out of reach.

Sarah worked extremely hard at school. She passed all her exams with great grades. She got into a top university and worked very hard throughout her time there. She hardly went out and put all her time into making her assignments perfect. When she left university, Sarah got a good job with the company she wanted.

Then the recession hit, and Sarah was made redundant. She suffered very high anxiety levels because she thought constantly about what she hadn't done perfectly and why she was made redundant. She felt like a failure, but Sarah had done nothing wrong. The company made her redundant because she was a new graduate with less experience than others, and graduates were the first group of people to be hit. It had nothing to do with the quality of her work.

Accepting yourself as already perfect

Instead of striving for perfection by relying on external factors, try accepting yourself as you already are! Underneath your anxiety, thoughts and worries, you're already perfect! You were born perfect but may have learnt negative conditioning, perhaps in childhood.

The stories in your head that you listen to about yourself aren't necessarily true. Your being is whole, perfect and complete just as you are. No one can be perfect all the time in that sense, but everyone is perfectly imperfect. If everyone was always perfect and everything was executed perfectly all the time, the world would be so boring!

Here are some suggestions to help you on the road to accepting yourself:

- ✔ **Begin with a sense of purpose to look after yourself using kindness and acceptance.** Looking after yourself first isn't selfish. In fact, you're better able to look after others in the future.

  Think of the preflight demonstration on a plane. Flight attendants always tell you that in the event of an emergency you're to fit your oxygen mask first, before helping any others with you, including children: If you start to run out of oxygen while struggling to fit someone else's mask, no one gets helped. But if you fit your mask first, you can receive the life-saving oxygen and then help others receive it, too.

  In the same way, when you show compassion and kindness to yourself, you're in a better and stronger position to show it to others. People may also learn from your example and begin to be kinder to themselves, too.

- ✔ **Write down a list of things that you like about yourself.** These items can relate to your physical appearance or the fact that you're a good listener or a good friend. Write down anything that comes to mind, even if it seems insignificant. This exercise is about accepting aspects of yourself, just as they are.

- ✔ **Discover how to forgive yourself.** Try to understand that you can't be perfect in what you do, and no one can get everything right 100 per cent of the time. See whether you can use your mistakes as a way of growing and learning.

If you still struggle with perfectionism, try being good enough instead of perfect. Try to accept that there is no such thing as perfection, but there is such a thing as good enough, and that can be achievable.

'I'm surprised you remembered to meet!'

I have a friend who's extremely forgetful. Sometimes when we meet up, I ask him to bring something for me. He nearly always forgets. When I ask him whether he's remembered and it becomes apparent that he hasn't, we start laughing because it's such a common occurrence.

I accept that he's forgetful, and he accepts that he's forgetful without beating himself up over it. He's a friend who's flawed just like everyone else. I accept him just as he is and enjoy his company when I see him.

Discovering Compassion for Yourself and Others

The word *compassion* literally means 'sympathy for the suffering of others often with a desire to help'. If you're practising compassion for yourself or others, you first need to be aware of the suffering. When you have no concept of just how hard other people's experiences can be, you're more likely to ignore them when they are upset or crying, for example, and therefore show no compassion.

To show compassion is about being moved by people's suffering so that you feel their pain in your heart. You want to reduce their suffering. By doing so, you feel a sense of warmth, caring and understanding towards them.

Compassion is about feeling warmth, not just the difficult feeling that you or others are experiencing. In that sense, it's different to empathy.

When you show compassion, you demonstrate a sense of common humanity. You understand that suffering, failure and errors are part of the human experience. You're much less likely to judge people severely on their errors or failures.

Being compassionate towards yourself

You may have difficulty showing compassionate to yourself. Common misconceptions about self-compassion may get in the way, such as the following:

✔ **Motivation:** People sometimes mistake self-compassion for self-indulgence and are worried about what they may allow themselves to do. Perhaps you think that if you feel upset and practise self-compassion, you'd stay in all day, watch bad TV and eat junk food! Although behaving in this way is okay occasionally, if you do it regularly you're not showing self-compassion.

Self-compassion means looking after yourself and your happiness in the long term, not just the short term. It may mean going to the gym or giving up smoking for your health or cutting out the TV and getting earlier nights in bed. It may involve doing things that aren't necessarily instantly pleasurable but knowing that the result will be long-term benefits.

✔ **Self-pity:** In fact, self-pity is egocentric and doesn't allow thoughts of compassion toward anyone else. Self-pitying people think that they're the only ones in the world with their problems and exaggerate them. They often stay stuck in the victim role. They become incredibly self-obsessed and separate themselves from the world around them.

In contrast, self-compassion allows you to see how you can relate to other humans in their suffering and see things through a more balanced view. You're more able to put things in perspective and understand that even though what you're going through is tough, other people may be in a worse situation.

I've had trouble with my knees since I was a teenager. After one nasty fall, I became very upset about the pain and my situation. I started to feel sorry for myself. A bit later, I thought about all the people in wheelchairs or who're paralysed, whereas I can walk. I berated myself for feeling sorry for myself initially. But then I started being self-compassionate, allowing myself to move through what I was feeling, without trying to suppress my emotions, just being aware and observing them as they came up. I practised the loving-kindness meditation (see the earlier section 'Understanding Loving-Kindness'). The next day I felt a lot better, with a more positive outlook.

Ask someone you trust or feel close to, such as a friend, to write down three good things about you. Then, write three good things about that friend. These attributes can be about physical appearance, aspects of personality or even habits that you like. Read these three things to each other and see how you feel.

Showing compassion towards others

Studies show that compassion and kindness toward others helps boost your happiness. It does so by making you feel happy with where your life is at, giving you a sense of connection, helping you relate to others and reducing stress. It can help stop you from thinking about your own troubles and provide a sense of purpose and meaning in your life.

Also, the more compassionate and kind you are towards others, the more likely you are to spread it around. Compassion is contagious, creating a happier community around you.

You can get involved in being kind and compassionate toward others in a number of different ways. Being compassionate doesn't have to mean a giant gesture; it can be something as simple as making someone's life a little easier by eliminating a day-to-day chore.

Here are a few ideas to get you started:

- ✔ Cook a surprise dinner for a partner or a friend.
- ✔ Volunteer for a local charity of your choice.
- ✔ Read to, offer to shop for or perhaps just visit an older person for a chat.
- ✔ Send someone you haven't seen for a while a random surprise present. (It doesn't have to be expensive, but if you can't afford it, send a nice quote or poem.)

> ✔ In a coffee shop, pay for your drink and then pay for the person waiting behind you.
>
> ✔ Let someone go in front of you in a supermarket queue.

Also keep in mind these wise words:

> *If you want happiness for an hour, take a nap.*
>
> *If you want happiness for a day, go fishing.*
>
> *If you want happiness for a year, inherit a fortune.*
>
> *If you want happiness for a lifetime, help someone else.*
>
> —*Chinese proverb*

Sometimes, however hard you try, you're unable to change things. In this situation you need to take a step back, start being kind and compassionate to yourself and accept things as they are. The serenity prayer is a great reminder and asks for the following:

> *The serenity to accept the things I cannot change;*
>
> *The courage to change the things I can; and*
>
> *The wisdom to know the difference.*

Chapter 7

Journeying from Excessive Anxiety to Mindful Wellbeing

*I*n this chapter, I describe what your journey may be like from suffering anxiety towards a more mindful way of living. I give you tips and tricks to help you on your journey, methods for supporting yourself and also how to enlist the help of others along your way.

I use the metaphor of a journey because mindfulness isn't a quick fix and takes time to integrate into your life. Mindfulness may not reduce your anxiety in the short term, but it certainly offers a way of living despite your anxiety in the long term.

Starting anything new is always tricky, but with the right support, understanding and motivation to carry on, mindfulness can help you on your journey to greater wellbeing.

Starting the Journey at the Edge of the Forest

If you're going for an adventurous walk through the forest, you can plan it in many different ways. You may prepare yourself with maps and compasses, or you may not have a planned route and just want to see where the journey takes you.

Try to see your anxiety as normal because everyone experiences anxiety on some level to a certain extent. You need to ask yourself whether you want to continue on your journey as you are (suffering with anxiety) or consider a different way of travelling – that is, meeting up with anxiety and living with it, which is mindfulness.

All sorts of different types of travelling exist, and in the same way, you can integrate mindfulness into your life in many different ways. You may want to use this book on its own, or you may want to consider other resources that work alongside it:

✔ One-to-one coaching or therapy

✔ Online courses

✔ One-day workshops

✔ Group courses meeting once a week over eight weeks

When deciding how to manage your anxiety, make seeing a doctor your first port of call before you decide on starting any new form of therapy yourself. Then you can consult your health professional and with guidance choose how you want to proceed.

What you choose to do ultimately comes down to your experiences in the past, how you learn best and what you feel comfortable with. If you're happy just reading through the book and having a go at some of the exercises, that's perfectly acceptable!

If you've just experienced a major life event, such as bereavement, a marriage split, a house move or major surgery, now may not be the best time to start mindfulness. You need a bit of space and time in your life, so make sure that you allow for that before taking on such a valuable and important skill.

Seeing the wood despite the trees: Difficulties along the way

When travelling through the forest, sometimes you can get stuck and just see nothing but trees obscuring the way forward. You may have become a little lost or are struggling to stick to the original plan. In these situations, you need to try to let go and just enjoy the adventure.

The same applies to your mindfulness journey. The less attached you are to things working out a certain way or to any ideas of how you think mindfulness should be, the more useful your experience is likely to be. New adventures and journeys always have some difficulties.

Often anxiety makes you want to avoid your anxious thoughts and feelings rather than experience them, but this approach is unhelpful because it doesn't assisting managing your anxiety. In fact, the efforts you make to avoid anxiety just make it more sticky and difficult to handle. Mindfulness shows you how to deal with difficult thoughts and emotions and loosen their power over you (as I describe in Chapter 4).

In all journeys, allowing for difficulties is a good idea. For example, on your adventure through the forest, taking a first-aid kit is sensible. You may need it if you have a fall or get bitten by an insect. In the same way, allowing for difficulties in your mindfulness journey is sensible. You may want to be aware of obstacles that you can face when beginning your mindfulness practice. Here are a few examples:

- ✔ Not enough discipline to practise
- ✔ Not enough time
- ✔ Not enough motivation
- ✔ Not understanding what you're doing

Being aware of possible obstacles before you begin can help you when you run into difficulty. You can accept them, manage them as best as you can and move past them.

Another difficulty is that mindfulness increases awareness, so your anxiety may feel more intense, especially at the beginning of your journey. The reason is down to you focusing on your anxiety rather than avoiding it, which is what being mindful is all about.

You may wonder why you're doing a practice that may increase your feelings of anxiety rather than lessen them! The subtlety of mindfulness for anxiety can be a hard one to get your head around.

Mindfulness is a radically different way of managing difficult thoughts and emotions. It isn't about getting rid of your anxiety; it's about making space for the feeling to 'be' and not identifying with it. Instead, you discover how to allow and accept the thoughts and feelings rather than fighting them. You find out how to face emotions gently and watch your thoughts for what they are — just images and words. This concept isn't easy to grasp and can be challenging.

Understanding the journey of a lifetime

Mindfulness isn't some kind of spiritual goal, a way of reaching a higher power or about achieving enlightenment. Beginning to practise doesn't mean that everything is going to work out perfectly in your life or that you'll achieve perfect peace and never encounter a stressful event again! But the fact that mindfulness doesn't have any specific goals is important because it means that you don't have to worry about achieving anything.

Ultimately, mindfulness is about discovering how to face the feeling of anxiety and continue to live your life, despite your negative thoughts and challenging emotions, in a kind and wise way. When you become mindful of your anxiety, you discover how to let it be. When you do that, you can continue to focus on what's important to you: your relationships, your work, your dreams and passions. Your life is about living in a fully present way and accepting whatever arises for you in a flexible and totally engaged manner.

Think of mindfulness as being about the journey not the destination, as you discover how to become aware of present-moment experiences in your day-to-day life. Mindfulness shows you how to experience life fully, moment by moment, thus increasing your levels of wellbeing and connection with the present moment.

Keeping a Journal to Strengthen Your Practice

Many therapists, social workers and other professionals in the health sector advocate writing a journal for greater wellbeing. In fact, some research shows that journaling can benefit your health, including

✔ Strengthening your immunity to minor viruses

✔ Improving your concentration

If you're stressed or anxious, sometimes the very act of writing down your thoughts and feelings can release them or help you get a clearer understanding of a difficult situation. It can help you pinpoint stress or anxiety triggers and so more effectively notice any patterns. Also, because the journal isn't a person and is nonjudgemental, you can write in an honest, open way and share as much as you like with 100 per cent confidentiality (fortunately journals don't tittle-tattle!).

Journaling can also help you stick to other activities that can help your wellbeing, such as a healthy diet, more exercise and better sleep.

Here are some suggestions for journaling:

✔ Try to write every day – aim for at least ten minutes if you can.

✔ Keep a pen and paper in an easily accessible place – such as next to your bed.

✔ Use the journaling time as a relaxing period – put on some music or write by candlelight if you like.

✔ Write whatever you want – no one has to see this journal except you. So, if you feel like sharing your innermost fears or most anxious thoughts, write them in your journal.

Writing to the rescue

As a teenager I went through some stressful events in my life. I had the telltale signs of anxiety: fast heartbeat, sweating and a feeling of too many thoughts being all tangled up in my head.

At this time, I was given a lovely notebook for my birthday. I used it to get the jumble of my thoughts out of my head and onto the pages and did so over a few weeks and months. I felt a lot better after my thoughts and feelings were on the pages and in a better position to cope with the stressful events that were happening to me.

Writing a journal to help your mindfulness practice

A great idea is to keep a journal just for your mindfulness practice. For example, you may want to write down your experiences after trying a mindfulness meditation, such as the sitting meditation (see Chapter 5). When you notice certain thoughts, discomforts or emotions, writing them down can help to prolong a mindful attitude of curiosity toward them.

Adopting an attitude of gratitude is also useful. When you write down everything you're grateful for each day, your happiness and wellbeing levels rise because you're focusing on the daily positives that you experience rather than the negatives.

Using the journal to monitor your progress

Keeping a mindfulness journal makes tracking your progress easier as you get deeper into your practice. You can use your journal to document your experiences of mindfulness in many different ways. Table 7-1 includes an example layout.

You can also use the journal to document how you feel about each mindfulness practice, as I show with the example in Table 7-2.

Table 7-1	Gratitude Diary
Day of the Week	*What I'm Grateful for*
Monday	Nice lunch, time spent with my children, my dog.
Tuesday	
Wednesday	
Thursday	
Friday	
Saturday	
Sunday	

Documenting your experiences can help you keep on track with your mindfulness practice, especially when you're finding that it has positive benefits for you. You may also want to keep track of your moods daily and perhaps a sleep diary to see whether you're having any changes as your practice progresses.

Enjoying the Vital Support of Other People

The support of the people you live with is important to help sustain your mindfulness practice. I don't mean that they have to join in with you or even understand what you're doing, just that they offer support in various ways. This support can range from actively trying to give you quiet time alone to meditate to not dismissing or demeaning what you're doing.

Asking family members to cooperate

In a busy working family, quiet time alone can be hard to find. However, when you first begin your meditation practice, noisy distractions can be off-putting.

Table 7-2 **Mindfulness Practice**

Mindfulness Practice	Observations	Difficulties	Thoughts/Emotions	Bodily Sensations
Sitting meditation (see Chapter 5)	I managed to focus on my breathing a little. My mind kept wandering off, but that's okay!	Finding it hard to sit still for any length of time	I became aware of a negative thought. I keep having about myself. I'm slowly discovering how to see thoughts as just thoughts rather than facts	Could feel some tension in my shoulders
Body scan (see Chapter 5)				
Breathing space (see Chapter 4)				
Loving-kindness (see Chapter 6)				

Ask your partner or an older responsible child whether they can keep younger children, pets and other distractions and responsibilities out of the way for your meditation period. This time can range from 10 to 30 minutes, so it may be challenging but not impossible!

Your partner or one of your children wanting to meditate with you is always welcome. It can help you stay motivated and focused when you feel that you have a support network at home.

As a beginner, distractions can be annoying, but if you really can't avoid them, try the following:

- ✔ **Open up your awareness and attention to the distractions for a while.** Instead of trying to fight the distractions, you're now using less energy and becoming mindfully aware of what's distracting you. After all, mindfulness is about developing awareness rather than trying to avoid difficulties.

- ✔ **Meditate for shorter periods of time, such as ten minutes a day, when starting out.** Also choose somewhere you're less likely to be disturbed.

- ✔ **Focus on the distraction.** For example, I'm writing in a quiet study room at the library, but next door is a baby-and-toddler group. Instead of trying to block out the sounds of the children, I'm practising mindful listening and noticing the sounds without judging them.

Gaining group support

Meditating in a group is beneficial and provides powerful support. You're more likely to stick to the discipline of meditating when you know that other people are doing it with you. Group support can also help if you feel your meditation practice is getting difficult or you're feeling less motivated than before.

Group meditation is different from the experience of meditating alone. Many people say that it deepens their experience when they meditate in a group.

Check notices in public places, such as doctor surgeries and libraries in your area, for mindfulness groups. Mindfulness is becoming increasingly popular, and I've seen notices for mindfulness groups in several community buildings. Also check out Chapter 10 for more on mindfulness courses of all sorts.

If you can't find a mindfulness group in your area, consider starting one! You can do so with interested friends or strangers; all you really need is just one other person.

Keep your group meetings simple and friendly. Here's an example itinerary of a simple mindfulness meditation group:

1. **Arrive and welcome all newcomers.**

2. **Try some mindful stretching.**

3. **Carry out a formal mindfulness meditation, such as the sitting meditation or the body scan (see Chapter 5 for details).**

4. **Allow people to share their experiences if they want to.**

5. **Socialise and share some healthy refreshments if you want to, such as grapes and herbal tea.**

6. **End the group meeting.**

For the formal meditation in Step 3, practise for 30 minutes or so. Perhaps play a guided audio meditation or ask someone to read out a mindfulness script. Don't forget that you can shorten or lengthen the meditation depending on your audience.

I coached mindfulness to a family with teenagers. I adapted the meditations for them because they thought that the teenagers' concentration wouldn't stretch to 30 minutes. I broke the meditations down into 15-minute chunks. The sessions went swimmingly!

Part III

Applying Mindfulness Every Day for Anxiety

Common anxiety conditions

Here are four common anxiety conditions and their symptoms, which can all be at a level that is difficult to deal with:

- ✔ **Generalised Anxiety Disorder (GAD):** Symptoms are restlessness, feeling constantly on edge, a real sense of dread, difficulty concentrating on anything and irritability.

- ✔ **Social Anxiety:** Symptoms may include a sense of dread when talking to strangers, talking on the phone, starting conversations, group activity, a massive fear of being criticised, being unwilling to make eye contact or just a fear of one particular situation.

- ✔ **Panic Disorder:** Symptoms include nausea, vomiting, trembling and a sensation that your heart is beating in an irregular way

- ✔ **Obsessive-Compulsive Disorder (OCD):** This affects people in different ways. It usually has four steps: obsessive thoughts or urges in the mind, anxiety, a compulsion to think or repeat a behavior and then some temporary relief. Obsessive thoughts and behaviours can range from mild to severe.

Find out more about Managing Anxiety with Mindfulness at www.dummies.com/extras/managinganxiety.

In this part . . .

- ✔ Discover how to live mindfully each day.
- ✔ Learn how developing healthy habits can help with anxiety.
- ✔ Find out more about the practice of mindfulness.

Chapter 8

Living Mindfully Day-to-Day

*O*ne great advantage of mindfulness is just how easily you can incorporate it into your everyday life, helping to improve your work life and relationships as well as boost your daily wellbeing.

In this chapter, I explain how to bring mindfulness exercises to your regular daily activities. The benefits include a better work life, including even your commute, and also improved intimate and nonintimate relationships.

Engaging in Daily Mindfulness Meditations

Mindfulness essentially cultivates an awareness of the present moment, which you can apply to most things that you do on a daily basis. As your mindfulness practice deepens, you find that doing these daily activities allows you to engage more with everyday life. This experience deepens your enjoyment and connection of your life.

Drinking tea mindfully

You can even drink a cup of tea mindfully. This practice gives you a little break and time to check in with yourself.

Usually, when you drink a cup of tea, you are not present. Your thoughts take you away to all that is going on in the mind (for example, Planning and worrying).

If you feel that your levels of anxiety are too much to cope with a full-length sitting or body scan meditation (see Chapter 5), this exercise can be of great benefit to you.

Most people drink tea on a daily basis for a break at home or at work, so you can easily fit it into your schedule. The idea is that you fully focus on the task in hand, so try to take the time to drink the tea alone or somewhere you won't be disturbed.

The tea-drinking mindful exercise is meant to offer a break and isn't a chance to keep going with work or multitasking, so ensure that you give yourself a real tea break! Ideally, use herbal or decaffeinated tea or decaffeinated coffee, but you can also apply mindfulness to other drinks, such as a hot water and lemon or even adapt it for a cold drink.

To practise the tea-drinking meditation, follow these steps:

1. **Place your tea bag in your cup or mug and add your hot water.**

   Listen to the sounds of the water as you pour it into the cup and watch any rising steam. Notice any smells that are released from the tea bag as the hot water fills up the cup.

2. **Sit down somewhere comfortable to drink your tea.**

   Find a situation with a nice view, if possible.

3. **Hold the cup of tea in your hands.**

   Feel the warmth of the cup. Notice the weight of the cup and any special designs on it. Feel your breath as you wait for the tea to cool down.

4. **Bring the cup slowly to your lips and take a sip.**

   Be aware of how the touch of the handle feels on your fingers or on your palms if you hold it with both hands. Smell the scent of that tea as you touch of the edge of the cup with your lips

Become aware of the flavours and the warmth of the tea on your tongue and the back of your throat. Notice the tea inside you, travelling down toward your stomach.

5. **Note when your mind wanders off.**

If your mind wanders, just gently guide it back to focusing on your tea-drinking. Be kind to yourself as you do so, allowing yourself a little smile.

6. **Take a moment after you finish your tea.**

Be grateful that you made the time to practise this exercise, no matter how you felt the experience went for you.

Drink your tea slowly and reverently, as if it is the axis on which the earth revolves — slowly, evenly, without rushing toward the future. Live the actual moment. Only this moment is life.

—Thich Nhat Hanh

Making time for mindfulness in a busy lifestyle

Getting into a new routine (such as daily mindfulness practice) is always difficult, but it's not impossible. You adapt to new routines all the time. Getting up for school or work, exercising, eating and watching a favourite series on TV are all routines that you had to learn at some stage.

Formal meditation

Remembering to fit into your daily life the longer formal meditations – those for which you have to make time – can be challenging in the hurly-burly of jobs and responsibilities. Here are two suggestions to help you:

✔ **Set a daily alarm:** Whenever you decide to practise, set reminders on your phone or computer. Although you can easily say to yourself, 'I'll meditate tomorrow', a noisy reminder helps you stick to your practice!

✔ **Place reminders wherever you see them every day at home:** Reminder notes, such as on your bedroom mirror or noticeboard, and other visual prompts can be very useful to you.

Ask yourself the following question to help you get into your new daily mindfulness routine for formal practice: What time of day is best for you to practise?

✔ When you've just woken up

✔ Mid-morning

✔ Before lunch

✔ After work

✔ When you arrive home

✔ Before dinner

✔ Before bed

Think about your answer and choose whichever time is easiest for you. Set aside at least 20 minutes a day for formal practice if you can. If you can't manage this amount, try breaking it up into two sets of ten minutes a day.

The important thing is to incorporate formal mindfulness into manageable amounts of time. For example, you may feel disappointed if you plan to practise for hours but can't attain that level of commitment with a family to look after. Be realistic with expectations and remember to be kind to yourself!

Don't practise formal mindfulness immediately after a heavy meal. Leave at least half an hour to an hour after you've eaten.

Informal meditation

In contrast to formal meditations, informal mindfulness doesn't need such a large time commitment. Instead you incorporate it into your existing daily routine.

Informal mindfulness involves daily activities that you can do mindfully, such as the drinking tea exercise in the preceding section. Chapter 11 has more great examples. Remember to focus fully on the activity, note why you're doing it and place your attention on the task as much as you can.

An example daily informal mindfulness exercise is preparing breakfast. If you're doing this while holding a mobile phone to your ear and watching the television at the same time, you aren't performing the task mindfully! On the other hand, if you focus on the smells and textures of the food – gently guiding your attention back to the task in hand when your mind wanders – and let go of any self-criticism as much as you can, that's mindful.

Incorporating mindful eating into everyday life

Eating is something everyone does every day to stay alive, but eating habits are different: Some people stick to three square meals a day, and others like to snack. Whatever your eating habits, you can bring mindfulness to them.

Think about your daily eating habits. Ask yourself the following questions:

- ✔ Do you eat at your desk at work?

- ✔ Do you eat in front of the TV at home?

- ✔ Do you eat or snack on the go, such as rushing to work or somewhere else?

If you answer yes to any of these questions, you have an opportunity to change your eating habits to be more mindful.

Here are some suggestions to help you to incorporate mindful eating into your daily life:

- ✔ Take a lunch break away from your desk somewhere quiet for at least 15 minutes.

- ✔ Turn off the TV at dinner time and fully focus on your meal.

- ✔ Leave enough time to eat meals and snacks so that you can stay still and not rush.

- ✔ Set a timer when eating a meal to gauge whether you're being mindful or racing through it.

✔ Have a meal in silence with your partner or family at least once a week to help you to focus on the activity of mindful eating.

✔ Eat with the opposite hand to the one you usually use. This change sends a message to the brain that something is different, and it can help you focus.

✔ Before you start your meal, practise gratitude for a few moments for the wonderful food you're able to consume.

✔ Chew your food about 20 times before swallowing it, if you can. Soup is obviously not applicable here! Doing so slows down your eating habits, helps you to be more present and can help your digestion, too.

It helps to put your utensils down while chewing between bites.

Try these suggestions and incorporate the mindful eating exercise from Chapter 5 into each one of them. You can bring mindful eating to any food, whether it's a snack or a big meal. Just adjust the mindful eating exercise accordingly.

Cultivating a joyful commute

Commuting, especially in a busy city, can cause unnecessary stress and anxiety. The city is crowded with a lot of people all trying to get to the same area, tensions can rise and stress can build among large groups of people in one place.

Mindfulness can help.

✔ **Let go of getting anywhere fast, whether you're travelling by road, rail or other means of transport.**

Most cities have huge transport systems, but they often have problems and a lot of traffic. Allow good time for your journey and set your alarm earlier if you have to.

But remember that you can't ultimately control the outcome even with the best-laid plans. You may encounter extra traffic due to roadwork, cancelled trains due to unforeseen circumstances and delays. Try to adopt the mindful attitudes of patience, acceptance and letting go. Getting stressed and anxious in these situations doesn't help move the traffic or make the train arrive.

✔ **Be mindful of the feelings in your body as you do your commute.** Be aware of any tension you may be holding in your legs while standing on a train or tension in your shoulders waiting in traffic. Be curious and kind toward your bodily sensations and try to be as nonjudgemental as possible.

✔ **Be aware of your surroundings.** You may have some nice scenery to look at out of a train or car window, or you may be sharing your journey with other people whose faces you can notice. Be aware of your thoughts and emotions as you do so. If you get caught up in a heated moment with another commuter, take a few moments to breathe and try sending a little loving-kindness to the person (see Chapter 6) – if you can manage it.

Everyone's in the same commuting situation as you, but they may handle it very differently.

Maintaining Positive Relationships

Relationships and the way you interact with other people can have an effect on your health. Cultivating quality relationships makes you feel happier and more secure and gives you a greater sense of purpose.

Being with friends and family

A lot of people want to make more time to spend with family but never get around to it. Family time is very important, and spending time with friends and family can make you feel supported, able to share your feelings and receive emotional support, which you can also give in return. Such relationships also boost your feelings of self-worth, belonging and being connected.

If your anxiety prevents you from enjoying social activities, practising mindfulness can help you manage your feelings and emotions in social situations. You can then be open to socially connecting with more people and making friends. Quality is better than quantity, so make friends with a few people you feel you can trust and enjoy spending time with. You should be able to feel like you can confide in these people and that you can see them regularly.

If you feel anxious in the presence of a certain friend, you may decide not to spend too much time with that person. Instead, spend time with friends or family members who empower you, especially when going through a bout of anxiety.

Sustaining positive relationships with colleagues

Colleagues are people you see every day and have to work with, sometimes very closely. No one in the office or your place of work has to be your best friend if you don't want them to be. But you see these people on a regular basis, so maintaining good relationships with them is important for your own mental well-being and comfort at work.

Here are two suggestions to help you with your relationships with work colleagues

- ✔ **Practise loving-kindness:** Include work colleagues when you practise the loving-kindness meditation (see Chapter 6). When you get to your place of work and you see them, try thinking or saying to yourself 'May you be well, may you be happy'.

- ✔ **Change your perspective:** Everyone has a slightly different perspective on life than you do, and no one is perfect.

  For example, you may feel that your boss is a little unfair. But his managers may put pressure on him to get certain things done, so he's trying to do the best he can and has to curtail certain freedoms. Or you may find the girl who sits next to you quite cold, but she may have had a difficult childhood and has difficulty relating to people with a sense of warmth. Considering such possibilities can help you feel more compassion and become a bit more forgiving.

Dealing with Difficult Relationships

No doubt you've had at least one difficult relationship in your lifetime. It's very common and nothing to be embarrassed about. The following list covers some techniques to help you handle relationship difficulties a bit more mindfully:

- **Practise regular meditation.** Just as meditation can help you become aware of your bodily sensations, it can also help lower your stress response the next time you encounter the difficult person. It can stop you reacting automatically and defensively and help you make wiser decisions when responding to that person.

- **Move towards your difficult feelings.** A lot of unhelpful emotions and thoughts can arise when you see the difficult person. Try to allow them to just be there instead of fighting them. Avoiding such thoughts can make them stronger whereas allowing them can disempower them.

- **Think about all the positives you can in relation to that person.** Even though you may find it challenging, that person has some positive qualities, so try focusing on them. For example, a parent may irritate you by quizzing you constantly about your personal life, but that person may also always be present for you when you're upset or going through a difficult time.

- **Remember that people aren't their behaviour.** If you make a mistake or shout at someone or behave in an inappropriate way once or twice, that doesn't mean you're a bad person. Perhaps you had a bad day or became frustrated and expressed it in an automatic way. Such reasons may apply to another person's behaviour as well, so try to be aware of that the next time someone behaves difficultly toward you.

Handling problems with a significant other

Anxiety can be challenging in partnerships because it arouses suspicion, evokes neediness and causes jealousy. Mindfulness helps to improve intimate relationships, however, giving you a chance to react constructively rather than automatically. It allows you to take a step back from any unhelpful thoughts and be able to stay in the present moment more so that you spend less time worrying about the future of your relationship or what may go wrong.

For example, just because your partner gets home late a few times a week, it doesn't mean that an affair is the cause. Even if this has happened to you in the past, mindfulness can make you aware of your brain's negativity bias and realise that thoughts aren't necessarily facts.

Here are some mindful ways to communicate with your partner:

- Before you know that you're going to see the person, do a short meditation, such as the breathing space (see Chapter 4), to help ground you.

- Be aware of the other person's body language. What does the facial expression tell you? Is your partner happy or sad?

- Practise mindful listening when your partner talks. Listen to the tone of voice as well as the actual words. Try not to use conversations as a chance to get your opinion or side of the story in. Really engage with listening to what your partner is saying.

- Pause before you speak to allow you to respond in a better way.

- Be aware of your own voice when you talk. Do you sound calm and controlled or angry and harsh?

As mindfulness helps you become more aware of your thoughts, bodily sensations and emotions, you can start to recognise patterns in yourself and be aware of what's arising for you. You can evoke empathy and start to be kinder to yourself. This awareness has a knock-on effect and helps you show more empathy towards your partner as well.

Just as you are becoming more aware of how judgmental you can be toward yourself, try to be the same with your partner so that you are less likely to blame or criticize.

Intimate relationships need a lot of hard work and mindful communication. Talk over issues calmly with your partner to try to work through them. Sometimes, however, intimate partnerships don't work out. You don't need to be ashamed or think that you've failed. If you've tried mindful communication and talked over issues and things still aren't working out, you may decide to agree to go your separate ways. But see this step as a last resort and not a way to avoid any anxiety about partnerships.

Managing a daily workload mindfully

Mindfulness is the opposite of multitasking. Mindfulness is about focusing on one task at a time with present-moment awareness. It can help with the quality of your work because multitasking doesn't allow you to focus fully on each task you're doing.

To manage a daily workload mindfully, break it down so that it doesn't feel overwhelming. For example, if the first thing you do when you get into the office is to check and answer emails, set yourself a time limit — perhaps a couple of hours in the morning or afternoon. Otherwise, you can end up checking your emails all day as they arrive, which brings your focus away from other tasks you need to do that day.

Here are some more suggestions to help you manage your work mindfully:

- **Write a list of everything you have to do that day. Prioritize each task.** Between each task, include a mindful practice, such as the breathing space (see Chapter 4) or even a tea break, as I describe earlier in this chapter in 'Drinking tea mindfully'.

- **Do one task at a time with full focus.** Don't rush your work because it causes more mistakes and may take longer overall when you have to go back and correct it.

- **Don't be afraid to ask for help from others.** If you can delegate, do so that you can relieve some of the pressure on you.

✔ **Be honest with yourself and your boss or manager if you can.** If you're asked to take on more work that you don't think you can manage, and you have an opportunity to say no, say no. This is an act of kindness toward yourself. You don't need to be more overloaded than you can handle.

Still have fun with your work if possible. If you enjoy some of the tasks, make sure that you keep doing them as well.

Chapter 9

Changing Unhealthy Habits to Healthy Ones to Combat Anxiety

In This Chapter

▶ Avoiding stimulants and nonprescription drugs

▶ Cultivating mindful healthy habits

▶ Maintaining your motivation

*M*indfulness encompasses your mental and physical health, so small lifestyle changes can make a huge impact to your mood and your life. The healthier you are, the more you enhance your ability to tackle anxiety and get into the habit of practising mindfulness regularly.

You may not even be aware that certain habits are affecting your anxiety and mood – such as what food, drink and drugs you put into your body. In this chapter, I describe how you can turn unhealthy habits into healthy ones to help you better manage your anxiety.

Documenting the small changes you're making in your life and whether you notice any changes in your mood or anxiety is extremely helpful. This (positive!) habit motivates you and helps you focus on keeping your lifestyle balanced and healthy.

Cutting Down on Stimulants and Certain Drugs

 When you're anxious, your brain is already stimulated. The anxiety activates the stress hormone in your body, and you may be in the fight-or-flight response (check out Chapter 1 for details). The stimulants such as caffeine and nonprescription drugs that I mention in this section can be harmful, serving only to intensify such anxiety, so you should reduce or abstain from them.

Reducing caffeine intake with mindfulness

Caffeine is a stimulant. It increases your breathing and heart rate, which gives you a boost (the well-known caffeine kick). But if you're under stress or suffering from anxiety, you just increase your body's stress response with coffee, therefore making your anxiety worse.

As a stimulant, caffeine also keeps you awake. It stops the effect of adenosine, a chemical that lets the brain calm down.

 Getting adequate sleep is vitally important for anxiety sufferers, so cut out caffeine altogether if you can. If going cold turkey is too difficult, try limiting yourself to one or two cups a day of coffee and have them in the morning so that the caffeine doesn't affect your sleep.

 Many people find that when they're in the habit of drinking coffee, getting out of it is difficult, particularly if they've relied on it for several years to help them get out of bed in the morning. If you don't drink coffee (or indeed other caffeine-containing drinks) yet, best not start so that you don't have to stop later!

Mindfulness can help you become aware of your thoughts and therefore aware of your body's desire for caffeine. The body's urges tend to have a rise-and-fall effect, and people tend to submit to the urge when it's at its peak. When you feel the desire for a cup of coffee, you can begin to bring a mindful awareness to your body's sensations and watch the urge as it falls away again after the rise, therefore not succumbing to it.

Think of the rise-and-fall of urges as being like a wave. The wave rises and rises until at its peak and then gradually comes back down again. Mindfulness allows you to watch the waves from a safe distance, instead of being caught up in them (and getting soaked through). This is often called *urge surfing*.

This is a great exercise to try out to help manage your urges to take in caffeine. The same principles can be applied for any other addiction.

1. **Close your eyes and take a few deep breaths.**

2. **Become aware gently of any thoughts that are arising for you as you feel the urge for caffeine.**

3. **Move your focus and awareness softly to any emotions that you notice.**

4. **Notice any bodily sensations you may be having.**

5. **Bring a sense of kindness to yourself, your thoughts and your bodily sensations.**

6. **Accept whatever arises for you, saying gently to yourself 'I'm going to be kind to myself for my health'.**

7. **Open your eyes slowly.**

Reducing the use of harmful nonprescription drugs

Research shows that many illegal substances can have a detrimental effect on mental health and worsen anxiety. Even drugs that may appear safe, such as marijuana, can trigger panic attacks.

Regular use of cannabis affects the hippocampus – which isn't a big-headed, short-legged animal at university, but the part of your brain you use to develop new skills. Therefore, cannabis affects your ability to learn a new practice, such as mindfulness, as well as any other study that you may want to undertake.

Cocaine can bring about panic attacks and in some people cause severe anxiety with withdrawal. Ecstasy can bring about anxiety, too, and is a very dangerous substance to someone's mental health when mixed with another drug, such as LSD, for example.

Some of these drugs may give you a temporary lift or help you relax, but they're very dangerous in the long term. They can cause dangerous addictions and have a detrimental effect on your mental health, anxiety and finances. If you find that you have urges for some of these drugs, try out the exercise for caffeine in the preceding section. If you find these urges very strong and overwhelmingly difficult to control, seek help from a doctor or medical professional as soon as you can.

Choosing to drink less alcohol

Sometimes your anxiety can seem overwhelming and hard to manage. You turn to alcohol when you feel that you need it to be able to cope with a stressful or social situation. But although one or two drinks may take the edge off, alcohol doesn't help you deal with your anxiety in the long term – it's a form of avoidance rather than management.

Although alcohol may make you feel more confident and more alert at the time, it's a depressant and can have an adverse effect on your mood. After you've been drinking, the alcohol can affect your sleep and leave you dehydrated, feeling unwell and lacking in energy and motivation.

Mindfulness meditation struggles to help you when you're under the influence of alcohol or illegal substances. Cut out alcohol altogether if you can, but also have a look at the guidelines on the NHS website at www.nhs.uk/Tools/Pages/Alcohol-unit-calculator.aspx for how many units you can consume safely.

Looking after Yourself Physically

Mindfulness and physical health go hand in hand. In fact, mindfulness can aid your physical health by getting you to be compassionate to yourself, recognising negative patterns and therefore choosing to engage in healthy mindful habits.

Exercise, diet and sleep can all help manage your anxiety.

Moving your body mindfully

Exercise is very important to your mental and physical health. It boosts endorphins and serotonin (the happy hormone). It helps you increase your focus, sleep better, have a better mood, maintain a healthy weight and lessen your risk of developing some chronic diseases. In fact, if you exercise regularly, your risk of developing type 2 diabetes, stroke and heart disease is dramatically reduced.

Most of the mindfulness meditations I describe in this book involve sitting or lying down, mainly still. But bringing mindfulness to everyday physical activities is important as well, including exercise. So in the following practice, I show you how to be mindful while swimming.

I chose swimming because it's a low-impact activity on your body and protects the joints from stress and strain, which is particularly useful if you have any injuries. Ellie Simmonds, the British Paralympic swimming champion, says swimming can raise well-being levels up to 20 per cent in just one session!

If you don't know how to swim, use this exercise as a guide for any other physical activity, such as cycling, badminton, tennis or squash or even slow walking (I also describe such an exercise in Chapter 11). You can even bring mindful attention to activities such as cleaning the house or mowing the lawn!

Try this exercise to make your swimming experience more meditative than just physical movement:

1. **Begin with a few mindful breaths.**

   Feel the sensation of your breath as you stand at the side of the pool.

2. **Allow yourself to notice your body and what it feels like.**

   Can you feel any tension anywhere? What thoughts are going through your mind? How are you feeling?

3. **Get into the pool and become aware of the feeling of the water on your body.**

   Is it cold or warm?

4. **Become aware of your limbs as you start to swim.**

   What do your bodily sensations feel like? What does your body feel like to float?

5. **Continue to feel your bodily sensations as you move through the water.**

   Just swim as best as you can and let go of any outcome you wanted to achieve.

Creating a healthy diet

A healthy diet is good for you for lots of reasons. It can boost your immune system, give you energy, stop you from getting sick and help prevent against cancers and other serious diseases. It can also help with anxiety and depression.

A healthy diet doesn't mean that you can never allow yourself a packet of crisps or a bar of chocolate again! It means having a balance between eating healthy food most of the time and a treat sometimes.

The 80/20 rule is a good way to remember this guidance. For 80 per cent of the time eat well and then allow yourself a treat for the remaining 20 per cent.

For example, for six days of the weeks eat healthy meals and then allow yourself some treats on the seventh day, such as a chocolate bar or a takeaway.

Lots of information is readily available online and in books for healthy meal plans and what a healthy diet comprises. Here are a few guidelines to get you started:

- **Stay hydrated and drink plenty of liquids, ideally water.** Drink 1 to 1.5 litres a day or eight glasses.

- **Eat plenty of fresh fruit and vegetables.** Aim for five or more a day. For example, you can get several of your five a day by making a tasty morning smoothie.

✔ **Get plenty of protein.** Vegetarians can get protein from nuts, seeds, pulses and eggs. Meat eaters can find protein in fish and other types of meat as well.

✔ **Consume foods that contain vitamin B$_{12}$ and other vitamins and minerals, such as vitamin C, D and minerals like iron and calcium.** Avoid eating too much processed food and food that contains a lot of sugar, such as ready meals, fizzy drinks and sweets. Sometimes additives or preservatives in food can affect your mood.

Getting into a regular sleeping pattern

Some people manage to drop off immediately and sleep heavily for hours, whereas others find falling asleep difficult and have disturbed nights. Whatever your tendency, getting enough sleep can be a vital step toward managing your anxiety.

Falling asleep and staying asleep

Try these general tips to help you sleep:

✔ **Go to bed at the same time every evening.** This helps to get your body into a routine and deepens your sleep. Once in a while, it's okay to stay up late, but if you go to bed at different times every single night, it can lead to sleep problems.

✔ **Make your bedroom as quiet, dark, cool and comfortable as you can.** Use earplugs if the surrounding sounds are too noisy or a bedroom fan if you feel too hot when sleeping. Invest in black-out curtains to keep your room dark or alternatively sleep with an eye mask.

✔ **Keep your bedroom as uncluttered as possible.** Having a cluttered environment can cause a cluttered mind, so don't put off that clearout!

✔ **Try not to work in your bedroom if you work from home.** Ideally, use the bedroom only for sleep and other fun nocturnal activities – something to keep in mind!

✔ **Don't sleep during the day.** Limit naps to 10 to 20 minutes if you absolutely have to take one. These short power naps work best in the early afternoon when there is often a post-lunch dip in energy.

✔ **Exercise for 30 minutes a day.** But don't do it too close to night time because it can energise you instead of relaxing you.

✔ **Have a warm bath and drink some warm milk before bed.** But avoid having too much liquid before bedtime because it disturbs your sleep if you have to wake up to use the bathroom.

Overcoming insomnia with mindfulness

Mindfulness can help you reduce your stress and constant worrying, which makes it a great tool for overcoming insomnia.

Here are some mindful exercises to help combat sleep problems:

✔ **Practise mindfulness meditation or mindful movement before bedtime.** Use meditations or exercises, such as yoga, that are more relaxing than energising.

✔ **Focus on your breath if you're lying in bed unable to sleep (see Chapter 3).** Take a few deep breaths and then gently expand your awareness to any bodily sensations you may feel and any sounds you can hear. Bring curiosity and acceptance to these sounds and sensations as best you can.

✔ **Practise the body scan if you tend to wake up during the night (see Chapter 5).** Many people find that this meditation relaxes them.

✔ **Count every time you breathe out.** Start from one and when you get to ten, start again from one. Place a hand on your tummy to feel the breath, if it helps you.

If you still have difficulty sleeping, don't worry about it and don't make sleep an ultimate aim. If you manage to meditate all night, that's great! You still get some benefits from that.

Avoiding Overuse of Technology at Home

Although technology has many benefits, taking a break from it is also useful. Computers, mobile phones and TVs can all halt relaxation and the chances of being in the present moment because your brain is overstimulated with information.

This section describes how technology can affect you and ways in which you can better balance your use of it for your own well-being.

Not watching TV last thing before bed

The body can take some time to come down from the effects of stimulation from TV, particularly from the light that the TV and other electronic devices give off, such as computers and game consuls. This light keeps the brain awake and delays the release of melatonin, a hormone that helps you get to sleep.

Leave an hour between watching TV (screen time) and sleeping in order to get the best night's rest. Also, watching negative TV programmes at night, such as the news, can also contribute to sleep disturbance. (For more information on the importance of sleep for tackling anxiety, see the section 'Getting into a regular sleeping pattern', earlier in this chapter.)

Turning off your computer and mobile phone early

Technology is great, but it pushes people to achieve the ultimate levels of multitasking in the hope of becoming more productive. The brain doesn't cope well with too much multi-tasking, and the stress hormone builds up.

When you bring work home with you, sometimes even checking just one email triggers the fight-or-flight response (see Chapter 1). If you're already anxious, it further exacerbates your anxiety. You're not in the present moment because your mind is on work tomorrow or something else entirely.

Check whether you can have a go at choosing a time in which to switch off your mobile and laptop and stick to it. Then do something relaxing in the evening, such as having a nice meal or reading a book. Be mindful of your urges to use technology and whether you can allow that desire to subside in its own time, instead of reaching for the phone or remote control.

Some people find that having a technology-free 24 hours is helpful, such as 8 p.m. on a Friday to 8 p.m. on a Saturday.

Motivating Yourself to Meditate

Getting into a new routine can be hard, but if you brush your teeth and shower every day, you can also get into a routine of meditation. The irony is that the benefits of mindfulness meditation can be highest in those very situations of a busy lifestyle when finding time to practise is most difficult. You're better able to cope with any stress and anxiety that arises, and you find that your focus and energy increases as well.

This section is about getting (and staying) motivated, doing it gradually and not berating yourself if you miss a meditation. Routine is learned, and although you may not be able to manage it straight away, step by step you can improve on your practice.

Taking things one breath at a time

Scheduling your meditations is helpful. Put a reminder on your calendar or your phone or a prompt online for the time of day you want to meditate. Start meditating for ten minutes twice a day or whatever feels manageable to you. Even just sensing your breath for a few minutes is a meditation and an invaluable present-moment awareness (check out Chapter 3).

Think about the environment in which you're meditating. Is it comfortable and quiet for you? Opposite where I live is a park, and I often see a man meditating quietly under a tree. Even if that's not suitable for you, you can create a little corner in your home or bedroom with some soft cushions where you can go to do your meditation. Just build up slowly and gently and do whatever works for you.

Forgiving yourself for the occasional slip

You don't stay motivated and stick with any new habit if you give up easily. Take things step by step and don't beat yourself up if you make a slip. Bring as much of an attitude of kindness and self-compassion for yourself as you can manage (see Chapter 6 for more on kindness). You've picked up this book so that's a great start already!

You're only human and every human on the planet makes mistakes. Ease off any pressure you put on yourself and go at a steady pace. Remember perfectionism feeds anxiety.

Rewarding yourself every so often

To maintain your motivation, you need to reward yourself when you do manage to stick to your healthy habits. For example, if you manage to turn off your technology early every evening, go to the cinema with friends, family or alone and enjoy a good movie. Just make sure that you take care of yourself with a reward and an attitude of compassion and kindness as much as you can.

I have to be very disciplined with my writing. I wake up early, do a little meditation, have a healthy breakfast and write for a few hours in the morning. After that, I sometimes reward myself by seeing a friend for a nice lunch or doing something fun in the afternoon. This approach helps to take the pressure off the striving to make myself write or meditate, and I can enjoy the process more as well.

Chapter 10

Taking the Next Step in Your Mindfulness Practice

. . . .

In This Chapter

▶ Finding out the level of your anxiety

▶ Exploring an eight-week mindfulness course

▶ Discovering helpful therapies and organisations

. . . .

*M*indfulness is a lifestyle rather than a short-term fix, and my hope is that this book provides you with the tools you need to get started with mindfulness and manage your anxiety a little better.

But anxiety is a complex condition that can appear in many different ways. You need to determine whether your level of anxiety requires you to see a medical professional or not. From time to time, everyone has some of the anxiety symptoms that I mention in this book – in many ways, they're what give people their little quirks and make them human! But as I discuss in this chapter, if you have several of those symptoms, they're at a disturbing or excessive level and are severely affecting your work and home life, you need to seek medical help.

This chapter is also about developing your mindfulness practice further, whether that's reading more on the topic, engaging in an eight-week mindfulness course or going on a retreat. In addition, I mention other therapies and organisations that are very beneficial for anxiety sufferers.

Determining Whether Your Anxiety Needs Medical Attention

You may just have mild anxiety occasionally and find that using self-help books and moving your focus onto other things helps you manage it. You may also have gone through a stressful event recently that caused anxiety, such as a divorce, starting a new job or place of study. Or you may have suffered the loss of a loved one or moved to a new area where you don't know anyone.

Anxiety developing in these life situations is very common. The anxiety may be short term and eventually fade away. This book is designed to help with such mild to moderate anxiety.

But some anxiety is more serious. This section describes the symptoms of severe anxiety to help you decide whether you need to seek medical attention.

If you think that you have a more severe form of anxiety, consult your GP before undertaking any kind of self-help.

Looking at the length of time

Severe anxiety usually lasts for a period of six months or more. In that time, you're likely to have experienced symptoms such as chronic worrying every single day. If you have had this type of anxiety for that amount of time, visit your GP who'll want to know how you're feeling and probably ask about your home, life and work situations.

Even though talking to someone about your feelings and emotions isn't easy when you have severe anxiety, the more information you give, the better the doctor can help you and decide what treatment is best going forward. Your GP may also do some tests to check whether any other health problems exist that can also contribute similar symptoms, such as anaemia.

Considering the level of intensity

Severe anxiety can feel overwhelming and hard to handle. It may manifest itself in uncontrollable worrying in which the worries are extremely upsetting and stressful.

Here are four common anxiety conditions and their symptoms, which can all be at a difficult level to deal with:

- ✔ **Generalised Anxiety Disorder (GAD):** Symptoms are restlessness, feeling constantly on edge, a real sense of dread, difficulty concentrating on anything and irritability.

- ✔ **Social Anxiety:** Symptoms may include a sense of dread when talking to strangers, talking on the phone, starting conversations, group activity, a massive fear of being criticised, being unwilling to make eye contact or just a fear of one particular situation.

- ✔ **Panic Disorder**: Symptoms include nausea, vomiting, trembling and a sensation that your heart is beating in an irregular way.

- ✔ **Obsessive-Compulsive Disorder (OCD):** This affects people in different ways. It usually has four steps: obsessive thoughts or urges in the mind, anxiety, a compulsion to think or repeat a behavior and then some temporary relief. Obsessive thoughts and behaviours can range from mild to severe.

You may also have some of or all the physical symptoms that go along with anxiety, such as a fast heartbeat, an urge to use the toilet more often, a dry mouth and sweating.

If you recognise any of these symptoms and they're at an excessive level, the time has come to see a doctor. They can determine whether these symptoms are due to anxiety or some other cause. They can also make a more precise diagnosis and determine the right course of action for you – which may or may not be mindfulness-based.

Investigating the impact on your life and behaviour

Severe anxiety can affect your life in many different ways and impact on your relationships, home life and work.

Check out the following behaviours that can occur in people with severe anxiety:

- ✔ **Alone time:** You may want to be alone more often because you feel tired by the amount of stressful thoughts running through your head and want to try to manage them on your own. Similarly, you may want to stay only in certain locations, such as your home or place of work, and not go anywhere new or different.

  Anxiety can also make you needy and dependent. You may start to fear being left alone and not like your partner going out without you. You may also become very tearful.

- ✔ **Compulsions:** When you leave home, you may engage in behaviours such as needing to turn the light switch on and off several times before you leave and having to start again if you're interrupted. You may obsessively check the door is locked or make sure that you don't step on the cracks in the pavement. You may feel that if you don't engage in these behaviours, something terrible will happen to your loved ones or family.

- ✔ **Self-medicating:** You may try to cope with the overuse of alcohol or illegal drugs. But although drugs and alcohol can block out stressful thoughts and anxiety temporarily, in fact they make them worse, creating a vicious cycle in which you become stuck.

Engaging in an Eight-Week Mindfulness Course

The eight-week mindfulness course or Mindfulness Based Stress Reduction (MBSR) was started in 1979 by Jon Kabat-Zinn at the University of Massachusetts medical school. It has been running for over 30 years and is used in a secular way in hospitals, schools, prisons and workplaces.

Research shows that an eight-week mindfulness course can create the following benefits:

- ✔ Reduction in anxiety of 70 per cent
- ✔ Reduction in anxiety for at least three years after the course is completed
- ✔ Reduction in anger, tension and depression

Discovering the eight-week course

You can pursue the eight-week mindfulness course in many different ways, but every approach requires a certain level of commitment. You need to be able to do the following:

- ✔ Have one or two hours spare in the week to read the material that goes alongside the course.
- ✔ Spare at least 30 minutes a day to practise your formal mindfulness meditations.

Mindfulness isn't like developing other skills. If you start to learn a martial art, how to cook or any new skill, and you get bored, you can just give up. But mindfulness works differently; it's about sitting with those feelings of boredom and accepting them rather than giving up. In fact, mindfulness encourages you to bring attitudes of curiosity and acceptance to your boredom instead of quitting at the first hurdle.

Also, mindfulness has no specific goals and is about being rather than doing. If you're learning a martial art, with enough practice, you can eventually be a black belt or equivalent. But with mindfulness, your experience is different every time, and no right or wrong way exists on how to meditate. The only achievement you have to make in the eight-week course is to ensure that you do the practices!

Mindfulness also involves learning about yourself rather than about external things. You discover how to watch your thoughts, experiences, feelings and emotions. In many ways, the concept is completely different from what you may be used to, so it can feel challenging at first. But the rewards outweigh that.

The eight-week course may not be suitable if you've just been diagnosed with bipolar, post-traumatic stress disorder or have severe anxiety, such as I mention in the earlier 'Determining Whether Your Anxiety Needs Medical Attention' section. Always check with a GP or health professional before starting.

Practising the course alone

Lots of support and resources are available if you want to practise the eight-week mindfulness course by yourself. The benefits of doing so are that you don't have to stick to any set times and can practise whenever and wherever you feel like it, in a comfortable setting such as your own home.

Motivation is a little harder when practising on your own, however, because you don't have anyone else except yourself to push you or rely upon. Therefore, I outline here some great resources in the form of audio and books to help you get started:

- ✔ *Full Catastrophe Living* by **Jon Kabat-Zinn:** Jon Kabat-Zinn was instrumental in bringing mindfulness to the Western world and developed the MBSR course. He bridged the gap between science and meditation and is a Professor of Medicine emeritus at the University of Massachusetts Medical School where he formed MBSR.

  Dr Kabat-Zinn wrote this book based on his MBSR course, and it provides a detailed eight-week practice schedule along with success stories and research findings. It also details how mindfulness can help with a wide range of problems from stress and anxiety to dealing with time pressures.

- ✔ *Mindfulness: A practical guide to finding peace in a frantic world* by **Mark Williams and Danny Penman:** Mark Williams is a professor of clinical psychology at the University of Oxford. He was part of a team of three who developed Mindfulness Based Cognitive Therapy (MBCT). Danny Penman is an award-winning journalist with a Ph.D. in biochemistry who found mindfulness meditation after becoming temporarily disabled after a nasty accident.

  Their book is full of practical, simple and powerful practices, which can help break the cycle of anxiety, stress, unhappiness and exhaustion.

✔ *Mindfulness Workbook For Dummies* **by Shamash Alidina and myself (Wiley):** The book is a practical guide to help you with your mindfulness practice. It includes areas where you can record your practice and document your thoughts, feelings and emotions as you work through your mindfulness journey.

The book includes an eight-week mindfulness course and sections on mindful parenting and mindfulness for children, as well as mindfulness for stress, depression and anxiety.

✔ *Calming your Anxious Mind: How mindfulness and compassion can free you from anxiety, fear and panic* **by Jeffrey Brantley:** Dr Jeffrey Brantley is a consulting associate in the Duke Department of Psychiatry and the director of the MBSR programme at Duke University's Centre for Integrative Medicine.

The book explains the body's fear system and how anxiety arises. It offers healing mindfulness practices in a step-by-step format with testimonials and explanations.

✔ **www.franticworld.com:** This website is for the book by Mark Williams and Danny Penman. It includes several guided meditations that are part of the eight-week mindfulness course.

✔ **www.joellemarshall.com:** I offer a range of guided mindfulness meditations, including the body scan and loving-kindness meditation.

✔ **www.tarabrach.com:** This is a very reputable website where mindfulness meditations are available.

Finding a course to join

Mindfulness is increasingly common, so mindfulness courses have become widely available. Finding a course near you means that you can mix with like-minded people and have the support and motivation to keep going and stay focused.

Here are several ways to find a course near you:

✔ Have a look at The Mental Health Foundation's excellent website, www.bemindful.co.uk. Input your postcode to look for your local courses.

✔ Speak to your GP, who may know about local courses.

✔ Check public buildings, such as libraries and community centres, to see whether they have any notices about mindfulness courses.

Locating a mindfulness coach or therapist to guide you

A range of mindfulness coaching is available online or in person. Coaching can help you if you're struggling to meditate by yourself or having difficulty getting motivated.

A coach can guide you through an eight-week mindfulness course and give you support and help along the way. If you're struggling or even just have concerns or worries, a coach can help you overcome them and continue focusing on your mindfulness practice. Have a search online for mindfulness coaches in your area.

I offer mindfulness coaching online and in person. Visit www.joellemarshall.com for more information.

Using Mindfulness with Other Forms of Therapy

Mindfulness can work well alongside many different therapies and medication. It can help you manage your medication and boost other forms of therapy.

Anxiety often has a number of related conditions, such as adult Attention Deficit Hyperactivity Disorder (ADHD), chronic pain, fibromyalgia and Body Dysmorphic Disorder (BDD). You may find that knowing how mindfulness can work with therapy for some of these conditions is very useful.

In fact, therapists themselves are recommended to practise mindfulness because they can cultivate self-compassion, experience less burnout and thus have a better connection with their patients.

Mindfulness can work alongside therapy to help with a variety of conditions and create helpful programmes. You may be able to find these programmes in your local area through a simple search online, or you may even want to do an online course. For the UK, you could search bemindful.co.uk for example. Alternatively, your doctor or health professional may have specific recommendations for you. Here are some examples:

- ✔ **Mindfulness-based Relapse Prevention (MBRP):** This eight-week treatment approach from the University of Washington helps people in recovery from addictive behaviour. It focuses on relapse prevention and teaches people how to observe cravings and urges.

- ✔ **Mindfulness-based Eating Awareness Training (MB-EAT):** This programme helps with mindless eating, emotional eating and overcoming the guilt and shame that comes from overeating. It promotes a healthy lifestyle and helps manage conditions such as binge eating, obesity and diabetes.

- ✔ **Mindful Awareness Programme for ADHD (MAPS for ADHD):** The course includes education into the impact of ADHD and specific mindfulness exercises and meditations tailored to those with attention issues or ADHD.

Using ACT for anxiety

Research shows that Acceptance and Commitment Therapy (ACT) helps to treat anxiety along with numerous other mental-health conditions. It works by trying to stop controlling your anxious thoughts and feelings (acceptance), living in the present moment (mindfulness) and then preparing a course of action for moving on alongside your core values.

The idea behind ACT is that when you allow yourself to accept your anxious thoughts and feelings, you can then focus on the present moment and start to take steps to live how you want to.

The research results for ACT are very promising. It's definitely worth trying.

Therapies that work for some people may not work for others because everyone has slightly varying anxiety conditions. A combination of therapies may work for you, or a combination of therapy and medication, or just medication or just therapy. Always consult your doctor.

Changing how you think: Benefits of CBT for anxiety

Cognitive behavioural therapy (CBT) is the most common therapy for anxiety. It features a combination of two elements:

- ✔ **Cognitive therapy:** Your *cognitive processes* are your thoughts, attitudes, mental images and beliefs. A therapist goes through these with you and identifies any thought patterns, ideas and thoughts that can trigger your anxiety. The aim is to try to change your way of thinking so that you avoid these negative ideas. The therapist also tries to help you make your thoughts more realistic and helpful toward you.

- ✔ **Behavioural therapy:** This element helps to change any behaviours that are unhelpful to you. For example, if you're very anxious, you may start to avoid certain places or things, which can exacerbate your anxiety. This behaviour isn't helpful because it increases avoidance instead of managing your anxiety.

  The therapist may gently guide you to face up to your fear and expose yourself to the place or thing that makes you anxious. You discover techniques on how to handle your anxiety, by gradually engaging in the activity that causes you anxiety, step by step.

These two techniques work in combination because how you behave is usually determined by how you think. Depending on your condition, the focus is more on the cognitive or the behavioural element.

CBT contains many advantages:

- ✔ You can sometimes find that it's as effective as medication or works in cases where medication hasn't succeeded.

- ✔ You can complete it in a relatively short period of time.

✔ You can access CBT resources through therapists, books and online resources.

✔ You develop skills in CBT that you can bring to everyday life to cope with a variety of situations.

CBT is different from mindfulness because it's about *changing* thoughts to change behaviour. In contrast, mindfulness is about *identifying* thoughts that arise in the present moment, seeing them as separate from you and being as nonjudgemental as possible toward them.

Although they are two very different techniques and approaches, Mark Williams, Zindel Segal and John Teasdale combined mindfulness and CBT to create Mindfulness Based Cognitive Therapy (MBCT). It's based on Jon Kabat-Zinn's MBSR programme (see the earlier section 'Engaging in an Eight-Week Mindfulness Course'):

✔ **Cognitive part:** Breaks down negative thought patterns and helps patients to recognise incoming thoughts and feelings that can trigger a repeated episode of a condition, such as depression.

✔ **Mindfulness part:** Focuses on becoming aware of the thoughts that the patient is having, but not becoming attached to them, and observing them without judgement instead of reacting and acting upon them. To this end, the programme uses mindfulness exercises, such as the breathing space.

Although MBCT was specifically created for people with depression, it's also been scientifically proven to help with other disorders. The benefits of MBCT on people with anxiety are

✔ Reduced insomnia

✔ Tendency to be less neurotic, less needy and have a sense of greater self-worth

✔ Less dependence on alcohol, caffeine and illegal drugs to manage anxiety

The intention is that participants come to see their thoughts as mental events that arise with and are fueled by anxiety or depressed mood, but do not have to be taken personally .They no longer relate from their thoughts but to their thoughts as objects of awareness.

To find out more about CBT and MBCT, take a look at the following resources:

- ✔ *Managing Anxiety with CBT For Dummies* by Graham C Davey, Kate Cavanagh, Fergal Jones and Lydia Turner (Wiley)
- ✔ *Cognitive Behavioural Therapy For Dummies* by Rhena Branch and Rob Wilson (Wiley)
- ✔ *Mindfulness-Based Cognitive Therapy For Dummies* by Patrizia Collard (Wiley)

Also take a look at www.mbct.com, which is written by the developers of MBCT. It includes a clear explanation of the program and where to find a suitable therapist.

Managing the use of prescribed medication with mindfulness

Some people overuse medication for anxiety or use it as an avoidance tactic. They may take medication every time they have to face an anxious situation, such as meeting a new person, leading a work presentation or getting through a difficult family situation. But this behaviour doesn't help long term because you're essentially avoiding the feeling of anxiety. A fear of anxiety is what continues to feed the anxiety in the first place. Ultimately, mindfulness is about discovering how to accept and make space within you for the feeling of anxiety rather than trying to constantly fight it.

Mindfulness allows you to manage your anxiety more effectively in such events. It's about becoming aware of your thoughts, stepping back from them and seeing anxiety as part of your experience rather than part of you. You can then regain control over your life and lose the reliance on having to self-medicate.

Using mindfulness to manage everyday stressful events means that you don't have to overuse your anxiety medication, but instead just use it as prescribed by your doctor or health professional. In some cases, mindfulness has proved to be better than medication at curing conditions such as insomnia.

Mindfulness can work well alongside prescribed medication and can help you if you decide in the future to reduce your medication slowly, too.

Always talk to your doctor if you're thinking about reducing or coming off prescribed medication. Coming off medications needs to be done slowly and gradually with a lot of help, advice and support; going cold turkey may cause side effects. Always make sure that you consult with your doctor before changing anything about your prescribed treatments.

Expanding Your Mindfulness Practice

If you really want to deepen your experience of mindfulness, consider going on a mindfulness retreat. This section offers advice on how to make a choice about whether you should go on a retreat, and which one is right for you, at this time.

The section also includes lots of great organisations that can support you through your experience of anxiety.

Taking mindful retreats to move forward

Retreats are a great way of engaging in mindfulness without the distractions of home and work life. You can fully focus with like-minded people, often in beautiful settings and locations.

Here are some benefits of a retreat:

- ✔ You can get away from any destructive habits that you're used to, such as arguing with a partner, placing too much emotional demand on someone, overworking or using illegal drugs or alcohol to try and suppress your anxious feelings.

- ✔ You can be with other like-minded people in an environment that's all about mindfulness: nonjudgemental, supportive and welcoming.

✔ You have no responsibilities for the time you're on the retreat.

✔ You can live in the present moment for longer than you would normally.

✔ You have experienced mindfulness teachers on hand to help and guide you through the practice.

A lot of really great mindfulness retreats are available to you:

✔ **www.learnmindfulness.co.uk:** Shamash Alidina has authored several books on mindfulness, offers coaching and holds retreats in some lovely locations. Check out his website for more details of the next mindful retreat.

✔ **www.gaiahouse.co.uk:** Gaia house retreats have a rural setting in southwest England and are mostly silent. You can choose to do a group retreat, a work retreat or a personal retreat, and they vary in length from a day to a week. The silence aims to deepen the practice of meditation, but the teachers speak to guide the practice.

✔ **www.amaravati.org:** Amaravati is a Buddhist association in north London and runs mindfulness events such as 'Mindfulness at Work'. If you're interested in mindfulness in the Buddhist sense, it's worth checking out.

✔ **www.plumvillage.com:** This retreat centre in southern France was founded by Thich Nhat Hanh, a Vietnamese Buddhist monk. He's one of the most famous teachers of mindfulness and was nominated for a Nobel Peace Prize by Martin Luther King. Not only do you do mindfulness formal practice, but Plum Village also encourages daily mindfulness practice, such as being mindful when you shower, wash dishes, eat breakfast and even use the toilet! The atmosphere is light-hearted and supportive, encouraging joy and peace in the community.

A retreat may not be for you at this point if you're suffering from severe anxiety and emotional distress, or have just been diagnosed with a mental-health condition such as clinical depression or post-traumatic stress disorder. You may need one-to-one support before experiencing a retreat. Consult your doctor or health professional before booking.

Discovering other helpful organisations

Many great organisations can give you round the clock support and advice, however you're feeling. If you want to discover more about your condition, you need someone to talk to or you want to research how different therapies can benefit you, all these organisations can help:

- ✔ **Anxiety UK (www.anxietyuk.org.uk):** A national registered charity that has been running for over 40 years. It was started by somebody with an anxiety disorder and helps people who've recently been diagnosed with, or suspect that they have, an anxiety condition. The charity offers one-to-one support, information and a range of services using external agencies as well. It can also help with specific phobias, such as fear of spiders or being in crowded places. In fact, the charity can help with any specific phobias that are holding you back from getting on with your life.

- ✔ **MIND (www.mind.org.uk):** A leading mental health charity in the UK. It offers an extensive range of support from counselling, crisis helplines and drop-in centres to employment and training schemes and supported housing. The charity supports over 250,000 people in England and Wales and works tirelessly to end mental health stigma and obtain equal rights for anyone who's encountered difficulties because of their mental-health condition. It offers tips on everyday living and mindfulness and has a mental health A-Z giving information and support. You can search for your local centre or check out the website.

- ✔ **NHS (www.nhs.uk):** The NHS website has a range of information about anxiety and anxiety disorders, covering GAD, social anxiety, post-traumatic stress disorder and panic disorder. You can read up about your symptoms, methods of support, treatment and finding out when to see your doctor.

- ✔ **The Samaritans (www.samaritans.org):** The Samaritans was started in 1953 by a vicar who wanted to reach out to people in need, though it's a nonreligious organisation. It provides a telephone service where you can talk to someone 365 days a year, 24 hours a day. The Samaritans doesn't keep any record of your call, and you can talk about anything that's troubling or disturbing you in a nonjudgemental and supportive environment. You don't have to be having suicidal thoughts to use the service and in fact the majority of callers aren't suicidal; they just need to talk their feelings through.

The Samaritans are listening. . . .

When you call the Samaritans, a volunteer answers your call. The person listens to you when you talk about how you're feeling. You may then be asked whether you're feeling suicidal and about other feelings you may be having. You can talk for as long as you want to and end the call when you feel ready.

You can contact the Samaritans as follows:

✔ Telephone: Call on 08457-909090. This method is best when you need to talk urgently.

✔ Email: At jo@samaritans.org.

✔ Visit: The Samaritans have several different branches across the UK and Ireland. Go to www.samaritans.org/branches to find your nearest one.

✔ Write: The address is on the website.

Part IV

The Part of Tens

Enjoy an additional Part of Tens chapter online at www.dummies.com/extras/managinganxiety.

In this part . . .

✔ Find out more about the effectiveness of these ten simple exercises.

✔ Ease your anxiety with these mindful attitudes.

Chapter 11

Ten Simple Mindfulness Exercises for Managing Anxiety

*M*indfulness doesn't mean sitting cross-legged and meditating in that position for hours on end. Those meditations do make up some of the practice of mindfulness, but you can also bring mindfulness to the simplest of everyday activities.

This chapter explores how you can be mindful daily with ten simple exercises.

Being Mindful in Nature

I was lucky enough to go to the New Forest in Hampshire the other day. Horses and cows had free rein to walk across the road whenever they liked, rows of trees went on for miles and miles and the sun was bringing out the flowers' beauty and colours.

Just being there, breathing in the air and walking along the edge of the forest, made me feel calm. Reconnecting with nature is a great way to rest your inner being, your deepest sense of self. Living in a city or town, you can all too easily get caught up in the busyness of city life and modern-day living.

If you do live far away from the country or from nature, here are some suggestions to help connect with nature:

- ✔ Keep plants in your house and water them regularly or get an allotment, if at all possible.

- ✔ Plan to get out of the city to the country on a break, if you can.

- ✔ Notice the trees on the streets on your way to work, the birds singing and the sun in the day or the moon at night.

- ✔ Take a moment to notice stars when the night is clear, if you can see them.

- ✔ Explore nature together with young children. Their natural curiosity may rub off on you as well.

- ✔ Spend time around animals or with a pet. Research shows that certain pets can boost wellbeing levels.

- ✔ Go to your local park and practice some mindful walking, if you can.

Most towns in the city have a local park where you can enjoy the trees while walking with mindfulness.

Carrying out a Mini Body Scan Meditation

This meditation is a shorter version of the body scan I detail in Chapter 5. You can incorporate it into your day in the morning when you first wake up or when you're lying down during the day for a short rest, for example.

Allow 5–10 minutes for this meditation:

1. **Place a hand on your stomach.**

   Become aware of your breath as your stomach rises and falls. Try to accept the breath as it is without forcing it.

2. **Imagine the breath going all the way down the body into both legs and both feet.**

   If you find this difficult, just bring a mindful awareness to both feet. What do they feel like? What does the contact feel like with the bed or the floor?

3. **Picture the breath rising up your body, from both feet and up the legs.**

   Become aware of both knees and any sensations there. Similarly, become aware of both hips when you reach that point.

4. **Focus your breathing and mindful awareness on your tummy area and lower back.**

   Become aware of any sensations, remembering to bring a sense of curiosity and acceptance as much as you can.

5. **Bring the breath and mindful awareness to your chest and upper back.**

   Remember if the mind wanders off, just gently guide it back to the breath and whatever you're focusing on.

6. **Guide your breath gently down both arms to the fingertips and back up to the shoulders.**

   Observe any sensations in the wrist and elbow as you go.

7. **Focus your awareness on the neck, slowly moving up to the head.**

   Become aware of facial expressions and any tension in your face.

8. **Bring a sense of gratitude for your amazing body.**

   Also, bring kindness toward yourself for taking care of your health in this way.

9. **Open your eyes gently.**

Trying out a Mini Sitting Meditation

Sitting meditation is about opening up your whole awareness. This short sitting meditation can help you manage anxiety in a few ways. (Check out Chapter 5 for more details and the full version.)

This mini exercise can be practised any time you have a spare few minutes. Read through the steps first and then have a go at practising it.

1. **Sit in a comfortable position.**

   Become aware of your breathing.

2. **Notice any sensations you can feel in your whole body.**

   Accept any aches and pains as best as you can. Bring a sense of curiosity to them. If it helps, try breathing in and out of the part of your body that causes you discomfort if you can imagine this.

3. **Notice any sounds around you.**

   Be aware of the volume, the pitch and the quality of the sound. Discover how your mind judges sounds. Notice the silence in between and underneath the sounds. Let the sounds come to you instead of reaching out for them.

4. **Become aware of any thoughts you're having.**

   Try not to become caught up in thinking. Try to distance yourself from your thoughts. Watch them arise and pass away, just like sounds do.

5. **Allow your attention to be open.**

   Notice whatever is strongest for you – sounds, thoughts, bodily sensations, emotions or even just your breathing. If your mind wanders off, gently guide it back to your breathing and then go back to your open awareness.

Breathing Mindfully

Mindful breathing is one of the most basic of mindfulness meditations, but that doesn't mean it isn't as useful or as effective as the others. Its great strength is that you can breathe mindfully anywhere. The practice usually lasts for about ten minutes, but you can practice it for as long or as little as you like.

To practise this meditation, sit in a comfortable, upright position:

1. **Close your eyes and focus on your breathing.**

   Choose where you can feel your breath best: perhaps the tummy, the back of the throat or the breath going in and out of your nose. Accept the breathing as it is without forcing it to be a certain way.

2. **Bring your mind gently back to your breathing.**

   Your mind may wander off, which is perfectly normal. Don't judge or berate yourself; just gently guide your mind back to the breath. Accept whatever arises for you without getting annoyed or frustrated at yourself.

3. **Open your eyes gently and notice how you feel.**

   Have a little stretch if you want and then carry on with your day.

Practising a Mini Loving-Kindness Meditation

Loving-kindness is a great meditation for yourself and others. It can help you improve difficult or challenging relationships and any anxiety that arises as a result.

You can find a full version of a loving-kindness meditation in Chapter 6. Here's a mini version:

1. **Lie down in a really comfortable position.**

   You can do so on the floor or on a bed.

2. **Place your hands on your heart and imagine a warmth arising from it.**

   Say to yourself, 'May I be well, may I be happy, may I be full of love.'

3. **Imagine people that you know, such as family and close friends.**

   Say to them, 'May you be well, may you be happy, may you be full of love.'

4. **Imagine everyone you know – friends, family, acquaintances, work colleagues, people you see every day *and* people you don't like.**

   Say to them, 'May you be well, may you be happy, may you be full of love.'

5. **Imagine everyone you know, plus every living thing on the planet.**

   Expand your awareness to as many living creatures and countries and populations as you can. Say, 'May we all be well, may we all be happy, may we all be full of love.'

Listening Mindfully

Sometimes people hear but don't really listen. They do so because they're on automatic pilot and thinking about what they're going to say or do next without listening to what other people are saying or to what's going on. Mindful listening is important because it helps you to connect, and it improves your relationships with other people. How many times have you had conversations with people where you thought they weren't listening to you and were just waiting for their turn to speak?

You can also adapt the following mindfulness of sounds meditation to listening to a conversation you're engaged in:

1. **Focus on your breath for a couple of minutes.**

2. **Open your awareness gently to all the sounds you can hear.**

3. **Notice how your mind is quick to judge the sounds that arise.**

4. Be aware of the volume, pitch and quality of the sounds as they change.

5. Notice the silence between and underneath all sounds.

6. Let the sounds come to you.

7. Rest your attention on any sounds you can hear.

Cooking Mindfully

Cooking can be a creative pastime, and mindfulness enhances your enjoyment of it. Have a go at cooking a recipe that you love, or one you want to try, and notice what the experience is like for you.

Get a list of ingredients for your chosen recipe and follow these steps:

1. Feel your breath and the sensations in your body before you begin to cook.

2. Experience the sensations in your body as you whisk, chop, beat or crack the ingredients you're using.

3. Notice the texture of the food change as you start to prepare the meal.

4. Look out for any smells and new tastes while you're preparing the food.

5. Eat the food mindfully with friends or alone, making sure that you notice any differences in taste or smell.

Chapter 5 discusses mindful eating in more detail.

Walking Mindfully

You can carry out any activity mindfully, even walking!

This exercise is a guide for slow mindful walking, which helps to get you to be mindful if you're feeling restless:

1. Stand upright in a stable position with your feet hip-width apart so that you're standing in a balanced position.

2. **Become aware of your breath.**

3. **Shift most of your weight slowly onto your left foot and notice how the sensations in your feet change.**

4. **Move the weight onto the right foot and notice any sensations there.**

5. **Shift the weight back onto your left foot so that almost no weight is on the right foot.**

6. **Lift your right heel slowly and place it heel-first in front of you, becoming aware of your weight shifting in the body.**

7. **Complete the step.**

8. **Begin again with the left foot, noticing the weight of the body shifting and all the sensations when you take footsteps.**

9. **Walk in this slow mindful way for ten minutes or so, or as long as you can.**

Stretching Mindfully

Mindful stretching is another great physical mindful exercise.

Do these movements as slowly as you can, because the purpose of the exercise is mindfulness, not stretching:

1. **Stand in a balanced upright position.**

2. **Feel your breath without trying to control it.**

3. **Close your eyes gently.**

4. **Raise your arms slowly to the sky and feel the stretch in your arms and back.**

5. **Bring the arms back down again to your sides.**

6. **Repeat Steps 4 and 5 three times.**

7. **Notice how your body feels after you finish your stretching.**

Cleaning Mindfully

Housework can sometimes feel like a real chore, but bringing a sense of mindfulness to it can enhance your enjoyment and give you a feeling of mastery when you complete the task.

Here are some ways to be mindful when cleaning.

- **Washing up:** Notice your breathing and take a few deep breaths. Feel the washing-up liquid on your hands or the sensation of rubber gloves. Feel the bodily sensations as you scrub the dishes and open your senses to the smell of the soapsuds and any sounds you can hear as you move through this activity. Notice any feelings, thoughts and emotions arising as you finish the task and everything is clean.

- **Scrubbing the bathroom/kitchen:** Take a few deep breaths. Observe the kitchen or bathroom before you start. Feel the contact of your hands on the sponge or whatever you're using. Open your senses to the smells of the cleaning product. Become aware of any sounds that arise, such as squeaking from scrubbing a surface or a noise from spraying a product. Feel the sensations of cleaning different surfaces. What do they feel like? Are they smooth or rough? When you finish, take a look around and observe your handiwork. What does it look like compared to before you started? What thoughts and feelings come up for you?

- **Vacuuming:** Observe your breath for a few minutes. Turn the vacuum on and listen to the sound it makes – the volume, quality and pitch. Begin vacuuming and feel the contact of the vacuum with your hands and with the floor. Become aware of all the sensations in your body as you vacuum the area. Notice your thoughts and feelings as you finish the activity.

Chapter 12

Ten Mindful Attitudes for Easing Anxiety

*Y*our attitude about something can change everything. In this chapter, you explore a range of attitudes that can help with your mindfulness practice and in daily life as well. After all, mindfulness is a way of living and not just a set of practices to do whenever you remember, and so using these attitudes on a daily basis helps you consistently.

All these ten attitudes overlap, and through mindfulness, you find that they help strengthen each other, leading to greater levels of wellbeing.

Here are ten mindful attitudes that can help to ease your anxiety.

Practising Present-Moment Awareness

In essence, mindfulness is a present-moment awareness. The more mindful you are, the more aware you are of your surroundings, your thoughts and feelings, any task at hand and any physical or bodily sensations.

If you're very anxious, being naturally aware is quite difficult. For example, you may not be aware of your negative thoughts, the tension in your jaw or any other physical or physiological sensations your anxiety is causing.

For example, when I was studying at university, I was feeling really anxious. I had lots of negative thoughts about the fact that I may not achieve a good grade. My shoulders and jaw were tense. Actually, all I needed was a few regular breaks and some fresh air to help recharge me, but my anxiety was stopping me from seeing that. Mindfulness helps you take a step back and see things as they really are.

Sometimes you may feel that you're hyper-aware of your bodily sensations and want to reduce that feeling. But if you look more carefully, you discover that the problem isn't your awareness of bodily sensations; the problem is your judgement of those sensations.

Mindfulness is about being aware of the physical sensations, for example, and letting go of the associated judgements. The key to mindful living is discovering ways to be with the present-moment experience, kindly and curiously.

When you have an attitude of awareness, you can recognise unhelpful thoughts and physical and bodily sensations. Through this awareness, you can then make choices of how you behave and react to things instead of it being automatic.

You can cultivate awareness with a variety of mindfulness meditations. The body scan is one that can help you become more physically aware of your body. Check out Chapter 5 for more information on these meditations.

Helping Your Beginner's Mind to Blossom

The *beginner's mind* is about seeing things for the first time with new eyes – taking habitual behaviours, thoughts, responses and so on that you've done before and looking at them as if for the first time, afresh.

For a young child, this state is natural, but as you become older and used to the surrounding world, you're less inquisitive and excited by everything. Mindfulness encourages you to relearn this beginner's mind and therefore become excited just by the very experience of being alive.

Here's a story about a university professor and a Zen master about the importance of beginner's mind:

> *Nan-in, a Japanese master during the Meiji era (1868–1912), received a university professor who came to inquire about Zen. Nan-in served tea. He poured his visitor's cup full and then kept on pouring. The professor watched the overflow until he no longer could restrain himself. 'It is overfull. No more will go in!' 'Like this cup,' Nan-in said, 'you are full of your own opinions and speculations. How can I show you Zen unless you first empty your cup?'*

—Zen Flesh Zen Bones: A Collection of Zen and Pre-Zen Writings, Paul Reps and Nyogen Senzaki (Compilers), Tuttle Publishing

Fill in Table 12-1 with some of your habitual daily activities. Notice what happens to them when you pay attention to them for the first time. I provide an example to get you started.

Table 12-1   Paying Attention to Your Daily Activities

Habitual Activity	What I Observed When I Did the Activity as if for the First Time
Taking a shower	I noticed that I usually think about other things when I'm in the shower, such as work and the day ahead. I enjoyed really feeling the warmth of the water on my skin and the smell of my shower gel. My skin felt a lot softer after this shower, too!

(continued)

Table 12-1 *(continued)*	
Habitual Activity	*What I Observed When I Did the Activity as if for the First Time*

Spotting Your Tendency to Judge

The human mind naturally puts judgements on everything. When you leave your house and walk down the street, you've probably judged several things before you even reach where you need to be. For example, you may pass building work and think that it looks messy, pass a garden and think that it looks pretty or pass people and make silent automatic judgements about them.

This behaviour is perfectly natural and mindfulness can help you become aware of your judging. You don't need to stop judging entirely; you need some judgement in your everyday life. For example, if you're a teacher and a student gives you a piece of work to look at, you have to judge it. The student needs to know what to improve upon so that he can improve.

Instead, mindfulness is about noticing the judgement as it arises without putting a judgement on the judgement! Becoming aware of this tendency helps you to realise when you're putting judgements on situations so that you can step back from them. It may also help you to see when you're putting certain judgements on your anxiety and whether that's having an effect on it.

For example, when you're meditating on your breath, you may be thinking, 'I'm breathing too fast. I must slow down. What's wrong with me? This is too hard for me. I must relax. I'm not good enough to be mindful.'

It's okay for your mind to judge. Mindfulness is about *noticing* the fact that your mind is judging, rather than taking those judgments as facts.

Self-judgement is normal among humans. Have you ever been referred to as your own worst critic? I know I have! Mindfulness helps you to spot your own self-judgements, go easy on yourself, and breathe and smile.

Considering Curiosity

A great attitude to cultivate is curiosity. If you're curious when learning something new, you're likely to get excited about the process. You ask lots of questions, research deeply and listen to everything that's related much more.

When you bring this attitude of curiosity into your mindfulness practice, you can help ease your anxiety. The more curious you are about the thoughts, feelings and emotions that cause your anxiety, the less overwhelming and frightening it feels.

Imagine that you're camping in a remote place. In the middle of the night, you hear a lot of noises. It's very dark, and you can't imagine what's making all the noise. However, you use your curiosity, get a torch and shine it all around your tent. You discover that an animal, perhaps a hedgehog or a badger, is wandering through your camping area, and it caused all the rustling noises. After you discover what the noise is, you diminish any fear.

In the same way, when you become curious about the sensation of anxiety in your body (noticing its shape and location), it becomes less scary and more like something to explore. You discover how to live with it rather than run away.

Opening up to Anxiety

Mindfulness is about being open to your inner and outer experiences. *Openness* is about stepping back from your experiences, but not avoiding them.

Stepping back is useful when you have difficult or disturbing emotions. With this sense of openness, you can discover that you don't need to believe everything you think, and in turn you can watch emotions come and go without feeling attached or stuck to them.

For example, say that you've got a doctor's appointment coming up, and you feel anxious about it. If you don't take any time to open up to your feelings and acknowledge that you're a bit nervous about the upcoming experience, you may end up replacing the feelings with unhelpful behaviours. Maybe you'll cancel the appointment, or overeat or get too busy doing tasks that aren't very important.

With this sense of openness, you're more equipped to deal with emotions head-on instead of using avoidance or oppression toward them. You can use these words: 'I'm not anxious, I'm observing anxiety. The anxiety comes and goes, but I remain an open observer – separate, safe and free.'

Developing Self-Compassion

Most people are their own worst critics. How often do you think you show compassion to yourself? A way to be more self-compassionate with mindfulness is to become more aware of self-critical thoughts, emotions and physical sensations. (Flip to Chapter 4 for more on mindful management of thoughts).

When you can see things in a wider context, you start to be naturally more compassionate to yourself.

I'm not good when I'm very tired. I can make mistakes and am sometimes a little grumpy! When I'm in this state, however, being mindful allows me to recognise it and make allowances for myself. Instead of getting annoyed at myself, I try to make sure that I get a good rest as soon as I can and start again the next day with a clearer perspective.

Pursuing Patience – without Rushing

Mindfulness isn't a quick fix, and you're unlikely to have peace, joy and relaxation every time you practise (sorry!). Like anything new, mindfulness takes time and development. In the modern world, achieving patience can be difficult, because people are so used to getting everything immediately, whether its food, communication or even commuting!

Try the following steps to help administer an attitude of patience and lessen your impatience:

1. **Think of a scenario where you become impatient.**

    Examples include waiting in line at the post office or in the supermarket checkout queue.

2. **Ask yourself, 'Do I always need to be impatient here?**

    For example, perhaps you can allow yourself more time to do your daily activities. If you're always busy, consider letting go of some of your tasks on your to-do list. Being too busy goes hand in hand with impatience. Practise this step when you're next in a situation that makes you feel impatient.

3. **Keep a diary of your experiences for 1 to 2 weeks, writing in it when you felt impatient and recording the thoughts and feelings that you had at the time.**

    Look for any patterns. You may discover that your impatience is more related to the state of mind you were in at the time rather than to any external event.

Operating with Optimism

An attitude of realistic optimism when practising mindfulness is very important. Your anxiety may have made you feel discouraged from trying new things or hopeless about finding a technique that works.

An attitude of optimism *isn't* a delusion that mindfulness is going to fix all your problems immediately. A delusional attitude causes disappointment and frustration with the mindfulness practice.

Optimism in mindfulness is about developing a willingness to try new practices and not becoming disheartened if they don't work immediately. It's about saying to yourself, 'Okay, this didn't work for me this time, but with time, patience and discipline, it may work in the future.' With optimism, you discover what works for you and what doesn't while maintaining a positive approach.

When you first learned to ride a bike, you can't do it immediately. You probably wobbled all over the road, fell off a few times and got some bruises, I know I did! But with time and patience and maybe your parent's help, you managed to get rid of your training wheels and cycle away on your own.

Like mindfulness, it took patience, discipline and an optimistic attitude.

Generating Gratitude

> *Gratitude turns what we have into enough, and more.*
> *It turns denial into acceptance, chaos into order,*
> *confusion into clarity . . . it makes sense of our past,*
> *brings peace for today, and creates a vision for tomorrow.*

—Melody Beattie

The brain is more malleable than people used to think, which is useful because it means that you can change any negativity programming you have. By practising gratitude regularly, you remind yourself of everything that's going well in your life, and your brain starts to think more positively. In turn, your wellbeing levels are raised.

Gratitude is well-known in positive psychology. Here are two ways to start practising:

✔ **Visualise someone still alive who helped you or changed your life for the better a few years ago and with whom you can easily meet up.** Write the person a thank-you letter, arrange to meet up and read them the letter face to face. Record how you really feel.

✔ **Start a daily gratitude journal.** Write down three things you're grateful for every day. They can be as small as someone smiling at you on the train or having a nice dinner with a friend. Try varying the three things each day. Build up your gratitude when you feel ready.

Research shows that gratitude can have an effect on lessening anxiety, especially combined with lots of rest and a good night's sleep (something that gratitude also helps with).

Experiment with doing your gratitude journal at different times of the day. If you're having issues sleeping, try doing it right before you go to bed.

Here are some more positive outcomes of gratitude:

✔ Grateful people are more forgiving.

✔ Grateful people are more likely to be less materialistic.

✔ Grateful people are more hopeful.

✔ Grateful people tend to focus on what they can learn from life rather than on the disappointments.

Allowing Acceptance to Grow

An accepting attitude is key to mindfulness practice, but can be a complex one to master. The major difficulty with practising acceptance is the common misconceptions that go with it.

Acceptance doesn't mean giving up. Often anxiety sufferers feel that if they let go, everything will fall apart. They can sometimes believe that if they let go of their anxiety, the very thing that's making them anxious is going to be made worse.

But acceptance isn't about complacency; it involves accepting your present-moment experience as it is right now. It doesn't mean accepting that the situation will be the same forever. You may find that using the words 'allow' or 'let be' is helpful.

When you have strong anxiety feelings, you quite naturally want to try to avoid them. In the short term, doing so may help, but in the long term, you can end up more frustrated.

When you're practising mindfulness, your mind naturally wanders off to a million other things, and so a sense of acceptance is useful here as well. Remember that your judgement of yourself has been conditioned and isn't natural. The more you judge yourself, the less room is left for acceptance.

Anxiety can be quite overwhelming when you first experience it. I have suffered anxiety in the past and found that my first responses were to avoid and try to rid myself of the anxious feelings. However, once I looked at my anxiety in a different way and began to accept it rather than fight it, I was better able to manage it.

Anxiety is something that everyone suffers from at some point in their lives at various different levels. It can be managed, and there is help out there. I hope you have found this book to be useful, and I hope you get to enjoy the many benefits of mindfulness, not just with managing anxiety, but for greater wellbeing overall.

Acceptance of what's in the here-and-now can be the beginning of transformation. See what happens if you let go and just accept (or allow) your anxiety feelings. But mindfulness doesn't involve practising with the hope that anxious feelings will suddenly disappear. It's about acceptance of the present moment with whatever outcome that may bring.

Index

About the Author

Joelle Jane Marshall is a mindfulness teacher who trained with Learn Mindfulness. She offers private coaching either in person or via Skype. She also offers corporate mindfulness coaching as eight week courses or one day workshops/introductions.

Jo offers drop-in mindfulness classes and a limited number of eight week courses across London and occasionally runs one day workshops in London.

Jo has been featured in *The Career Stylist's Inspiration Lounge* and has held workshops for Girl Summit alongside Childline and the NSPCC.

Jo is the co-author of *Mindfulness Workbook For Dummies*.

See all Jo's courses, workshops, audio and books at www.joellemarshall.com or email her directly on info@joellemarshall.com.

Catch Jo on Twitter at www.twitter.com/jomarshall2.

Dedication

I would like to dedicate this book to you, dear reader. If you are experiencing anxiety at the moment, I hope the exercises and meditations in this book help you to find comfort and peace.

Author's Acknowledgements

I would like to personally thank Ben Kemble for approaching me with this book and giving me the opportunity to write a book on an important subject that could help so many people.

Thank you so much to Iona Everson for her patience and understanding when I was recovering from knee surgery. I was quite unwell at that point and I am very grateful to her for giving me some extra time! The whole team at Wiley have always been helpful and supportive, so thank you very much, I am fortunate to have had such a great team.

Thank you also to Angel Adams for agreeing to be a technical editor on this book. Find out more about Angel Adams, a Chartered Clinical Psychologist, at www.drangeladams.com.

Special thanks to Shamash Alidina, who has been a fantastic mentor, answered my many questions and concerns and gave my chapters a quick once over for me. He has also given me unwavering support and continues to be one of my most positive and encouraging friends, so for that I am truly grateful.

A big thank you to Hamilton for driving me to and from the local library so I could hobble in on crutches and get big portions of my writing done. Thank you also for your support and encouragement, even if you had to pick me up after an hour or so! Thank you also to my extended family, especially my Grandma. She has always urged me to follow my heart and choose what makes me happy, so I am indebted to her for that.

Thank you also to my friends Fran, Angie, Becky, Jackie, Ishia, Serena, Dominique, Sarah, Hayley, Suki, Ben and Chevi. Their support over the last year has meant a lot.

Finally, thank you to you, dear reader. Without your support this would not have been possible.

Publisher's Acknowledgements

We're proud of this book; please send us your comments at http://dummies.custhelp.com. For other comments, please contact our Customer Care Department within the U.S. at 877-762-2974, outside the U.S. at (001) 317-572-3993, or fax 317-572-4002.

Some of the people who helped bring this book to market include the following:

Acquisitions, Editorial and Vertical Websites

Project Editor: Iona Everson

Commissioning Editor: Ben Kemble

Production Editor: Suresh Srinivasan

Proofreader: Kerry Laundon

Publisher: Miles Kendall

Take Dummies with you everywhere you go!

Whether you're excited about e-books, want more from the web, must have your mobile apps, or swept up in social media, Dummies makes everything easier.

FOR DUMMIES

A Wiley Brand

BUSINESS

978-1-118-73077-5

978-1-118-44349-1

978-1-119-97527-4

MUSIC

978-1-119-94276-4

978-0-470-97799-6

978-0-470-49644-2

DIGITAL PHOTOGRAPHY

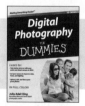
978-1-118-09203-3

978-0-470-76878-5

978-1-118-00472-2

Algebra I For Dummies
978-0-470-55964-2

Anatomy & Physiology
For Dummies, 2nd Edition
978-0-470-92326-9

Asperger's Syndrome For Dummies
978-0-470-66087-4

Basic Maths For Dummies
978-1-119-97452-9

Body Language For Dummies,
2nd Edition
978-1-119-95351-7

Bookkeeping For Dummies,
3rd Edition
978-1-118-34689-1

British Sign Language For Dummies
978-0-470-69477-0

Cricket for Dummies, 2nd Edition
978-1-118-48032-8

Currency Trading For Dummies,
2nd Edition
978-1-118-01851-4

Cycling For Dummies
978-1-118-36435-2

Diabetes For Dummies, 3rd Edition
978-0-470-97711-8

eBay For Dummies, 3rd Edition
978-1-119-94122-4

Electronics For Dummies
All-in-One For Dummies
978-1-118-58973-1

English Grammar For Dummies
978-0-470-05752-0

French For Dummies, 2nd Edition
978-1-118-00464-7

Guitar For Dummies, 3rd Edition
978-1-118-11554-1

IBS For Dummies
978-0-470-51737-6

Keeping Chickens For Dummies
978-1-119-99417-6

Knitting For Dummies, 3rd Edition
978-1-118-66151-2

FOR
DUMMIES®

A Wiley Brand

SELF-HELP

978-0-470-66541-1

978-1-119-99264-6

Mindfulness
978-0-470-66086-7

LANGUAGES

978-0-470-68815-1

978-1-119-97959-3

978-0-470-69477-0

HISTORY

978-0-470-68792-5

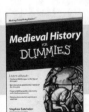

978-0-470-74783-4

978-0-470-97819-1

Laptops For Dummies 5th Edition
978-1-118-11533-6

Management For Dummies,
2nd Edition
978-0-470-97769-9

Nutrition For Dummies, 2nd Edition
978-0-470-97276-2

Office 2013 For Dummies
978-1-118-49715-9

Organic Gardening For Dummies
978-1-119-97706-3

Origami Kit For Dummies
978-0-470-75857-1

Overcoming Depression
For Dummies
978-0-470-69430-5

Physics I For Dummies
978-0-470-90324-7

Project Management For Dummies
978-0-470-71119-4

Psychology Statistics For Dummies
978-1-119-95287-9

Renting Out Your Property
For Dummies, 3rd Edition
978-1-119-97640-0

Rugby Union For Dummies,
3rd Edition
978-1-119-99092-5

Stargazing For Dummies
978-1-118-41156-8

Teaching English as a Foreign
Language For Dummies
978-0-470-74576-2

Time Management For Dummies
978-0-470-77765-7

Training Your Brain For Dummies
978-0-470-97449-0

Voice and Speaking Skills
For Dummies
978-1-119-94512-3

Wedding Planning For Dummies
978-1-118-69951-5

WordPress For Dummies, 5th Edition
978-1-118-38318-6

Think you can't learn it in a day? Think again!

The *In a Day* e-book series from *For Dummies* gives you quick and easy access to learn a new skill, brush up on a hobby, or enhance your personal or professional life — all in a day. Easy!